Courtney
You are on
your way
Serene!

Your friend,

What others are saying about this book:

"*How to Reprogram Yourself for Success* is an invaluable tool for tackling any issue in your life. I have used this technique with great success. The results have been astounding. Since I starting using these techniques my life has changed dramatically for the better. I recommend this book to everyone who wants to change their life!"

Jennifer Remling
Author of "Amazing Job Search Secrets"

"A good deal of what is in our brains is subconsciously programmed into us by our parents. Little things that apparently have no consequence can be an almost devastating block to the development of a fulfilled and empowering life. Thanks to Patrick Phillips for sharing the secret to the removal of these blocks in this special book."

Dr. Stephen Hudson, BDS, MFGDP
Master Practitioner
Neuro-Linguistic Programming

"Ever since CYBERNETICS, published in 1948, drew the analogy between human brain and computer we've been warned about Garbage In, Garbage Out. But how do we implement this wise advice?

"Short of policing every thought, we've had few tools. In this exciting new book you'll find fresh examples from other writers and in testimonials that show why this system is needed and how it works. Thank you, Patrick. You've done many people a service with your book."

Helen Shanley,
MA in transpersonal psychology
Author of "Dancing on the Sun:
Imagination and Reality"

"*How to Reprogram Yourself for Success* has enriched my life in every area. It has reshaped my way of thinking and has helped me to create a confident attitude for every situation I encounter. This book has taught me to focus on the positive and eliminate the negative. Thank you, Patrick, for making life fun and prosperous for me and thousands of others!"

Sue Robertson
President of Sue's Salsa

"Thank you for allowing me to review your book. The information is accurate and easy to understand, but the best part is that it actually works! The concepts you discuss in the book are the most important behaviors and thought processes needed for success in every area of life. Everyone should read this book."

Jennifer King HH Dip(M.P.Th.) TFT
Author of "Why Wait Until You Crash?"

"I have a deep appreciation for your authentic, practical and accessible message of empowerment delivered from your heart. I celebrate your noble effort and more importantly your tremendous concern to write with such a lean and concise style which reflects how much you care for your readers. You are obviously very interested in your readers succeeding in their quest to free themselves from negative thinking and elevate their lives by tapping into the infinite power within their minds. I will recommend this book widely."

Jesse Dean
Open Window Institute

"Patrick Phillips has added the missing piece of the puzzle. So many self-help authors take a simple concept and try to make it sound profound. Mr. Phillips has taken a profound concept and made its application so simple that a child could implement it. This book has me talking to myself in a new way already!"

Daniel R. Hardt
Author of "Daily Numeroscopes
and Applied Business Numerology"

"Don't let the size of this book fool you. It is packed with thought-provoking, practical and useful information for anyone who wants to create change in their life."

Dr. Nell M. Rodgers, DC, MN, RN

"Patrick Phillips does a great and convincing job of bringing the psychology of auto suggestion to a very easy to understand and practical level. The computer metaphor he uses helps explain why humans develop behaviors which can sabotage or lead them to success.

"His approach to reprogramming the mind is fast and effective. I recommend it to my clients, and use it myself to improve the quality of my own life."

Jose M. Baltazar
Counselor and Success Coach

"Many would consider the condition I was born with a disability. I have limited use of my arms and legs that results in a great challenge to dress, feed, and bathe myself. I can personally testify to the powerful techniques Mr. Phillips shares in this life-changing book. Because I have put these principles to work in my own life, I am currently the CEO of my own retail cosmetics/skincare company and I am also a professional motivational speaker. All this at the age of 21! Who says success has to come later in life? This book is a must if you want to learn how to embrace success and overcome challenges in your life."

Daniel Blackmon
Motivational Speaker
www.greatness-is-a-choice.com

"Those of us who have met Patrick Phillips know that he is a gem of a man. His book, *How to Reprogram Yourself for Success,* is also a gem—one that will discover and achieve your potential. Read this book. You'll be glad you did."

Dr. Gilles Lamarche
Author of "Steering Your Ship Called LIFE"

"In *How to Reprogram Yourself for Success,* Patrick Phillips has synthesized the essence of a complex issue and provided a powerful, yet simple solution. The wisdom of his experience combined with his insightful view of the human mind has allowed him to provide a blueprint for all of us to both change and take command of our lives. His book is a *must* read for anyone seeking to improve their lives and as well as those around them. I highly recommend you read this book and reach your true potential."

Stephen A Burgess, CEO
Business Toolbelt Inc.

"Patrick Phillips has enormously important things to say in this clear and convincing book. I believe he is absolutely on the money about the effect that our inner dialog has on us and how it can negatively affect our own lives. He offers a sound solution from his sweet heart and able mind, and I recommend his book with enthusiasm."

Brian Browne Walker
Author of "Be Happy Now"

"Thank you, Patrick, for solving the mystery that I have been obsessing about for years: why are some people very successful while others appear to 'settle' or simply do not take action? I have literally been 'giddy' ever since I finished reading your book because I finally *understand humans*! The mystery has been solved! *How To Reprogram Yourself for Success* is a must read and I highly recommend it to everyone who has a dream."

Ann Preston, CEO, Freedom Builders

"Throughout our lives we have both struggled with the negative belief that success only arises from those with a college degree or many years of experience. Since learning about the reprogramming methods that Mr. Phillips shares in this book we have collectively lost over 75 pounds, stopped biting our nails, are extremely confident in ALL aspects of life, and have completely wiped away the negative beliefs that held us back for over 20 years in reaching the success and financial freedom we now in our own business. Thank you so much, Patrick, for changing our lives forever, and helping re-program our minds and erase ALL negativity in our thinking. Our future is now in OUR hands. We highly recommend this book to everyone who comes across it. These ideas can and will change your life forever."

Les McDaniel and Cynthia McDaniel
McDaniel Cash-Flow and Billing Solutions

How to
Reprogram
Yourself
For Success

Patrick Phillips

Global Publishing Company
Fort Worth, Texas

Published by:
Global Publishing Company
8436 Denton Hwy.
Ste. 208-141
Fort Worth, Texas 76148

http://www.howtoreprogram.com

Unattributed quotations are by Patrick Phillips.

ISBN, print ed.   0-9742699-0-5
ISBN, PDF ed.   0-9742699-4-8
ISBN, audio ed.   0-9742699-6-4

Printed in the United States of America

Library of Congress Cataloging-in-Publication Data

Phillips, Patrick
How To Reprogram Yourself for Success / Patrick Phillips
Includes References and Sources
1. Self-help
2. Psychology

Contents

Change your thoughts and you change your world.

Norman Vincent Peale

Acknowledgements

My wife, Linda, has been my inspiration for more than 36 years, motivating me to make sure my own mental programming stays on track, and allowing me to accomplish all my goals, financial and otherwise. Her steadfast love and support have carried me through the years, and have given me the time and motivation to finish this book. Thank you, honey, for standing by me through the years!

My children, Adam and Sarah, have made it easy for me to be the father to them that I never had. Their happiness and success in life has been my motivation for writing this book and sharing my thoughts on this subject with others.

I will forever be grateful to Dr. Shad Helmstetter and the influence his work has had on my life. The revolutionary new ideas I learned from his books have literally changed my whole outlook on life.

And last, but certainly not least, many thanks to my editor, Elise Sargent, who saw the vision I had to share my story with others and worked diligently to make my rambling thoughts readable.

We cannot always control our thoughts,
but we can control our words,
and repetition impresses the subconscious,
and we are then masters of the situation.

—Florence Scovel Shinn

Foreword

In writing *How to Reprogram Yourself For Success*, Patrick Phillips has done a great service for people who would like to get past the stumbling blocks of old mental programs. This is a book that will give you practical ideas and tools to help you change the mental programs that are holding you back right now, and add positive new programs that will help you move forward in the future.

Today, two decades after the concept of self-talk and reprogramming burst on the self-help scene, it would be hard to find a top motivational speaker or personal growth author who did not include the concept of positive reprogramming in his or her advice on how to "get better."

But Patrick has taken the concept well beyond the admonition that you make self-talk a regular part of your everyday life. He has lived what he talks about, using reprogramming techniques to move from living a life of limitations, to living a life of exceptional fulfillment and achievement. How he did this, he brings to life in the pages of this important new book.

As someone who learned to get past the negative programs he lived with for much of his life, Patrick is, himself, living proof of how self-talk can impact your life in countless positive ways. His success, and the freedom it brought him, kindled a resolve to bring the story of self-talk, and the other secrets he learned along the way, to the attention of millions of other people who have struggled to find personal success, but who have been held back by the self-imposed limitations that negative programming creates in all of us.

For many years I have received letters and testimonials attesting to the power of self-talk and reprogramming in the lives of countless individuals. But instead of writing a letter or a few paragraphs that attest to the benefits of reprogramming, Patrick embarked on a mission to tell the full story – not just the story of the positive changes in his own life, but how using the same techniques he used could create similar changes in anyone's life.

Of all of the personal growth concepts I have researched during the past thirty years, none of them has equaled the use of self-talk in its effectiveness. While I found and studied dozens of good ideas for personal change, it was clear that an understanding of how the brain actually works, neurologically, and the simple reprogramming techniques we now call self-talk, was the one foundational key that would make every other personal growth concept work better.

As Patrick will show you in the pages of this book, people from every walk of life now use self-talk techniques to effect real change – the kind that lasts. You can too.

As you read the inspiring and enlightening message that follows, keep in mind that in writing this book, Patrick stands

16

on firm, scientific grounding. The concepts he presents are based on medical and neurological research in the relationship between natural brain programming – the kind we grow up with – and the results you and I experience in our work, our relationships, and in every important behavior in our lives. The research proves the direct connection between the programs we received as children, (along with the programs we learned to give to ourselves), and every attitude we have, and every choice we make every day.

You'll find this book is easy to read and understand; it is not a medical book about the neurophysiology of the human brain. But grounded in medical fact, How to Program Yourself For Success shows you how any individual, who wants to get better – at anything – can use scientifically proven, but everyday techniques that anyone can do, to make significant and lifelong changes.

The great futurist, Robert Heinlein, once wrote that a perfect university would be a log with a student at one end, and the right teacher at the other. In this book, you are fortunate to have Patrick Phillips sitting at the other end of the log. He is a teacher of life-changing wisdom, and best of all, he teaches from experience.

As you read the clearly written ideas that follow, I encourage you to open yourself up to the possibilities that lie ahead. Use them, try them, and adopt them. Make these ideas a part of your life.

If there are some things about your life you would like to change or improve, if you follow the suggestions and recommendations that Patrick outlines, not only will you find they lead to positive changes in your life; they will lead to a better you.

Shad Helmstetter, Ph.D.

Preface

I came across a secret just a few short years ago that literally changed my life. At least it was a secret to me at the time. And, although it turned my life around 180 degrees, there is nothing new about this secret. It's been written and talked about since the early 1980's. I am convinced, though, that most people have never really grasped how important it is in our lives, and how to put it to work for us in an easy, practical way.

This wonderful secret can change your life, as it has for countless others that have put it to work in their lives. I have personally shared it with many other people and have seen with my own eyes how it can change the direction of someone's life within a short time.

And now, I want to share it with the world, by giving my own testimony as to how it worked in my life.

At the age of 45, I had accepted what my father had told me for the first twelve years of my life. Just after my twelfth birthday he left town with another woman and abandoned my mother, me and two brothers. Although he only moved as far as Las Vegas, and he even called a few times, I never saw him again.

He had never held a job more than a couple of years at a

time. So I guess it made him feel better to be able to convey to me and my brothers, by his actions and with words, this mind-set:

> "Wherever you are in life is where you will always be.
> Financially and socially, no one ever rises above
> their 'place' in life."

Oh, I don't suppose he ever said those exact words, but the way he lived and the words he spoke depicted his attitude; which always indicated that this is what he thought of his own situation—and that we could only expect the same in our own lives. Maybe it was just his way of justifying his failures, who knows.

In any case, for the next 30 years, I believed that. He had said it so many times that my brain just accepted it as fact. I mean, this was my *father* telling me this, not a complete stranger. It had to be true, right? To a child, whatever he hears from his father *must be true*, as he has no reason to doubt it. To him, a parent is the ultimate authority who knows all and cannot lie.

Whether it was true or not did not matter. My brain accepted it as truth. And, for most of the first half of my life, I'm quite sure I did everything I could to fulfill that "truth" that I had heard repeatedly—to make sure that what my father had conveyed to me would come to pass.

Fortunately, my mother, who worked two jobs just to put food on the table, gave me a great example of a good work ethic, and a moral direction that would help me in my career and family life for the next 30 years.

But it wasn't until I was 45 years old that I found the secret to overcoming all those negative thought patterns my dad had programmed into my brain while he was there.

In short, I learned that my father had lied. I *could* be more successful than he was. I *could* rise above not only his failures in his responsibilities to his wife and children, but I could also be more successful in my career and personal life. I could earn more money and make a place for myself and my family in society and in my community.

As soon as I put this secret to work in my own life, I started my own business which had revenues of over 10 million dollars for several years in a row; moved from a small cookie-cutter house we had lived in for 17 years to a large two-story custom-built home in an upscale neighborhood; traded our two worn-out "clunkers" for brand new luxury automobiles, and began making ten times what I had previously earned.

We paid off all our debts (six major credit cards, all charged to the limits, and a number of department store balances) and began to earn enough extra money to provide at-home care for my mom, donate to various causes dear to our hearts, travel the world, and literally buy whatever our hearts desired; all because I learned how to reprogram my brain for success and financial freedom.

I'm not saying that earning lots of money will solve all your problems or make you happy. This will be just one of the things that *will change* for the better as you apply this secret to your own life.

Your relationships will improve; you will be more focused and you will worry less knowing that your future is bright. You will learn how to develop your self-esteem, take control of your health and career, and literally improve every aspect of your life.

Sound too good to be true? It did to me, too. It's one of those deceptive little secrets that seem almost too simple to have any lasting effects. Read on, and I will tell you how I ran across this secret and how you can put it to use immediately and change your life for the better – permanently.

1

The Strange Secret
That Changed My Life

When I was in college, in 1972, I ran across a record album by the renowned motivational teacher, Earl Nightingale, called "The Strangest Secret." I used to listen to that album, and others by Mr. Nightingale, every morning as I got ready for school. He went on to be the founder of the world's largest distributor of motivational tapes and CDs, and his work continues to inspire people today.

Early in his career, he became curious as to why some people had so much, and others had so little. So, he made a study of the elements of success, and interviewed dozens of people who, he felt, had "made it"—financially, at least. He looked for people who had money, and that's how he defined success, at least for this particular study.

Let me just interject here that, even though I now teach people how to change the way they think about money, and show them how to make lots of money, I want my readers to know I don't define "success" as just "having a lot of money."

If my wife Linda, whom I have loved for over three decades, came to me a few years from now and said, "Patrick, you know, you've spent a lot of time helping others be successful, but you didn't spend enough time making our marriage successful, and I want a divorce," — I wouldn't care how much money I might have in the bank, or how much gold or stocks I might own. If that happened, I would consider myself a dismal failure.

But having money is one of the principal ways that most of us define success; this is why Earl Nightingale traveled all over the country and interviewed dozens of "successful" people who obviously had made a lot of money. These wealthy individuals all shared with him their "secrets of success."

Each of them shared a lot of good things with him about success, but in one way or another, they all mentioned one particular secret—one factor which contributed to the success of every single person he interviewed.

This factor involves only six simple words, so you have to let them sink in or you'll miss their import:

"You Become What You Think About."

Now you may be thinking, as I did, when I first heard those words, "What a joke! How could thoughts, which are electrical and chemical impulses in your brain, actually *make you into who and what you become* as a person?" It just didn't make any sense to me, at first, and it sounded like some sort of new-age mumbo jumbo.

In fact, I knew it couldn't be true, because, if it had been, I would have been a woman a long time ago! (You may have to think about that one for a moment.)

However, a few years later I ran across a similar statement made by Buddha back in the 4ᵗʰ century B.C. He said: *"The mind is everything; what you think, you become."*

And, later, I ran across a verse in the book of Proverbs, in the Bible, that seemed to carry the same message:

"As a man thinks in his heart, so is he."

Doesn't that say the same thing as what Earl Nightingale took many years of interviews and research to discover: *"You become what you think about?"* Let that sink in: "As a man thinks in his heart, so is he."

You'll see a number of other quotations, sprinkled throughout this book, that all say the same thing: this idea is nothing new.

But it was for me. And that's all that mattered.

As I pondered these statements over the years, I began to believe that I just might have stumbled upon a very important secret of success. What if—just what if—a person could take control of his or her life, and become the person they wished to be—*by simply taking control of their thoughts?*

What if we could change the things we didn't like about ourselves by simply changing the thoughts in our minds?

It seemed simple enough. But, from a practical standpoint, just how do we do that?

I learned the first part of the answer, by learning about

25

computers and how they work—at a time when no one else knew how. I'm basically just a self-taught computer nerd who happened to have run across the connection between computers and the human brain, and who successfully put that knowledge to work in my own life.

It worked so well for me, in fact, that I became a millionaire within just a couple of years after running across it. I'm still in a daze as I think about the drastic changes that came about as a result of applying this simple secret in my life.

But before I go into detail about it, I need to tell you how I learned the importance of programming in the real world, and how it helped me grasp the importance of this newly found secret as it applies to success in life.

I think you will agree, as you read my story, that the connection is real. And if it is true, then everything you have ever hoped about success and financial freedom are about to come true in your own life.

We cannot seek or attain health,
wealth, learning or kindness
in a general way.

Action is always specific, concrete,
individual, unique.

—**John Dewey**

2

How I Learned the Importance
of Good Programming

These days, everyone from schoolchildren to retirees know about, understand, and can use computers. But it hasn't always been that way. I had the good fortune to be part of that exciting world very early.

From the start, as I said, I've been self-taught on most of the things I know about computers. My "training" began when I was hired to work with Apple Computer in 1981.

My very own personal computer...

I'll never forget that first day at Apple's computer plant in north Dallas. I thought I had a tremendous future there, and I was so excited when a guy showed me around and showed me my office. There, on my desk, sat my very own Apple computer.

It seems hard to believe that it was so exciting to have a

computer on your desk, but you have to understand that back in 1981, there was not anyone who had a computer on their desk. The best any manager could hope for, at the time, was a good calculator!

And so I guess I looked a little too proud of my importance as I stood there staring at the brand new Apple III, because the guy that was showing me around said, "Patrick, don't be too overly impressed with yourself — even the janitor has one of these on his desk!"

I said, "*Really?*"

"Yeah, everybody here at Apple has a computer on their desk."

"What do you do with them?"

"Well, we play games on them when we get home with them at night." (Apple let employees check out their computers and take them home.)

I said, "No, I mean what do you do with them here during business hours?"

He looked at me like I was crazy. "Nobody has any *time* to learn how to use them here during work hours. We're working 70 to 80 hours a week and shipping those computers out the back door so fast that we have no time to learn how to use them."

Click! A light bulb went off over my head. I was in the right place at the right time and I could see the awesome potential in computers for someone with expertise when no one else knew what they were doing with them yet.

I knew computers would change the world— and I wanted to be a part of it.

I knew that if I could learn to do something useful on this new-fangled thing, I could assure myself a career in the computer industry for a long time to come. So, I would unplug everything at the end of the day, take it home and hook it up, and work until late at night learning how to use the various pieces of software installed on it.

I brought the computer back to work each day, and I eventually started creating things that were useful, like spreadsheets and reports and other documents. My boss seemed to be impressed with what I was doing. In fact, everyone was so impressed that they asked me to start teaching other Apple employees how to use their computers so they too, could produce useful business documents.

So that became my job at Apple Computer. Can you imagine anything more exciting? Right at the very beginning of the computer industry I was actually working for Apple Computer and teaching other employees how to use these wonderful new tools to be productive in their jobs!

I loved my job and thought I had a long and prosperous future with Apple. Everything was great for a little over a year.

Then, one day, they brought me into a little room.

I was about to get the motivation I needed to change my life for the better.

Have you ever been brought into a little room, unexpectedly? You know what I'm talking about? You think you have been doing a good job and you suspect they are bringing you into the little room to give you a raise or a promotion – or at least a pat on the back.

But then you hear the word "downsizing".

And your heart skips a beat.

Well, to make a long story short, I was about to become one of the unlucky downsized mid-managers when Apple decided to move their Dallas plant back to Cupertino, California, in 1983.

Anyway, these two guys in the little room were talking to me about downsizing and cost control, and how sorry they were, and that it was nothing personal, blah, blah blah.

It was just like a bad dream. Their words didn't seem to register. As I sat there trying to figure out exactly what they were talking about, it finally dawned on me that they were talking about me! I, personally, was being "downsized."

Now, I don't know about you, but for a man who is the sole "bread-winner" for the family, which I was at the time, this can be devastating to your ego. I mean, we're the ones in the family who go out and "kill the bear to bring home the meat", and we provide everything for the family, financially (if the wife stays at home with the kids, which Linda was doing at the time.)

I thought my life had ended.

So as I sat there trying to grasp what was happening, all I could think of was how I was going to tell Linda that I no longer had a way to provide for our family.

I began to get very emotional; my hands got sweaty and my

heart was beating very quickly. This was so completely unexpected; and, unless you have experienced it personally, you can't imagine how it feels.

Now, my throat usually constricts when I get nervous like that. So, finally, after about 10 minutes, since I hadn't been able to say anything, they looked at me and said, "Patrick, do you have anything to say?"

All I could say (in a squeaky, high-pitched, emotionally charged voice) was, "Well, I was just wondering if I could keep my office computer?"

They must have thought I had lost my mind.

They were looking at one another, like "What is *wrong* with this guy? Here we've just told him he doesn't have a job anymore, and he's asking if he can have his office computer – and sounding like Mickey Mouse!"

Anyway, I drove home, very upset, and when I walked in the door my wife could tell something was wrong; probably the tears running down both cheeks was a fairly big hint. Here is the dialog that followed:

Linda: "Honey, what's wrong?"

Me: "Well, I've got good news and bad news."

"Well, give me the good news first."

"Well, the good news is that I don't have to get up at five o'clock every morning and drive all the way to Dallas."

"Really? What's the bad news?"

"Well, the bad news is that when I finally do get up, I don't have any place to go."

"You mean you were fired, Patrick?"

"No, honey, I was *downsized*. Don't you know the difference?"

"Well, doesn't that still mean we won't have any money coming in?"

"Well, yes, I guess so..."

"Patrick, you were fired!"

"Oh ... hmmm ... I guess you're right."

"Patrick, what are you going to do now?"

How getting fired led to my eventual success.

Now I've been the entrepreneur type all my life. I mean, since I was 14 years old I've had some little business going – and, throughout our marriage I either had something going or was thinking about starting another business of some kind.

However, those of you who think of yourselves as entrepreneurs probably can identify with this thought: being an entrepreneur doesn't necessarily mean that a person is *making* a lot of money – it just means he has probably spent a lot of money!

And, the truth was that over the years, I'd spent a boat-load of money on different business ventures, trying to get a business started. But I had never made even enough to cover the expenses of starting up most of them.

We had been married long enough by this point that Linda could recognize that look in my eye. You know, the "I'm-gonna-start-another-business" look.

So, when she asked what I was going to do, I said, "Well,

I don't know, but I do know *this*—I'm never again going to let anybody bring me into a little room and tell me I don't have a way to make a living for my family!"

Bless her heart, her eyes got bigger and bigger as I spoke, so I thought I should come up with something that sounded good.

I finally said, "Hey, you know what? I like people and I like computers and I like teaching people how to use computers—so that's what I'm going to do. I'm going to teach people how to use personal computers so they can have the tool to become more productive in their lives."

Linda looked at me with such love—and pity—and said, in her sweet, quiet way, "Patrick, I think that's wonderful—but hardly anyone out there in the business world even *has* personal computers yet. How are you going to start a business based on teaching people how to use computers if no one has them yet?"

(Remember, this was in the very early '80's, and IBM had just entered the market with the IBM PC.)

I said, "Well, no one may have them yet, but you just wait and see; every employee in America will have one on their desk in a short period of time, and every one of them will need to know how to use it. And I'm going to be there to fill that need!"

So, that's when I started my own computer training and consulting company. And, for the next eight years I traveled all over the United States, teaching thousands of people at large corporations and even government agencies, how to use personal computers and how to use technology to better their lives.

Things were getting better—but I still had to struggle with the effects of the negative programming I had received along the way.

How I personally found out about Garbage IN, Garbage OUT

I was working for the Food and Drug Administration in 1986, at their research facility in Dallas, Texas. I had been contracted to write a computer program for them. It was a simple database, written in dBase III, and was not very involved.

In doing contract work for the government as an instructor, I had taught dBase to hundreds of government employees over the past few years, and was quite confident I could easily write a program that would track their research projects.

Little did I realize there is a big difference in just teaching the basics of software language, and actually *writing* a program that would work without problems of any kind.

At the time, though, I was certain that it would be a piece of cake. No problem. So, I plunged into the project with all confidence that it would be a simple task that I could complete in just a few short weeks. Then I could move on to work for other clients.

Three months later, I finally had a program that I thought was error-free. But as it turned out, I had not written the technical specs the way that they should be written prior to beginning a software project. Unfortunately, it was *after* I completed the program and delivered it to the FDA, that the program suddenly began manifesting some "undocumented features"—

better known as "bugs!"

As I began to reexamine the program, line-by-line, it became clear to me that it was not the fault of the software manufacturer—or the computer hardware. The bugs that continued to show up were *my* fault. And with that, the first essential part of the secret was mine:

With computers, the results you get are only as good as the programming you've put in.

If the lines of software code contain the wrong information (as slight as a missing comma), the program will sometimes, under certain circumstances, perform in a peculiar and unexpected way. The computer simply carried out the (garbage) instructions, and did something that was not what the programmer intended (garbage).

Because of bad programming, the project I had thought would be so simple, took much more time and effort than I ever thought it would. And in spite of having reached a level of success in my career, the same thing was continuing to happen in my own life.

When it came to figuring out how to change, I was part of the way there—but I had to learn the second half of the connection between computers and the brain. It wasn't the initial programming that was important – it was learning how to erase and replace the old programs with new programs that could make the difference in someone's life.

And, boy, did it make a difference in mine.

You are searching for the magic key
that will unlock the door
to the source of power;
and yet you have the key
in your own hands,
and you may make use of it
the moment you learn
to control your thoughts.

—Napoleon Hill

3

The Breakthrough of Reprogramming

Throughout the time I was working with computers and learning how they work, I had continued to read, study and work on self-improvement.

I had purchased dozens of books, from *How to Win Friends and Influence People* to *Think and Grow Rich*. All classics. All with good ideas for improving yourself. But none of them contained the one thing that is necessary to put them into action in a person's life.

It was clear to me that I needed to change my thought process if I ever wanted to reach the level of success in my life I was striving for. But I still didn't know quite how to accomplish the changes, much less in a lasting way. I tried many methods, but after awhile they all stopped working, because my old programs of failure were still in charge.

The missing link, that would eventually provide a solution for me and for everyone else, came from an entirely different field of research than the computer world. The next part of the answer would come from the field of neuroscience—the study of the human brain.

The second part of the secret: Your brain is like a computer.

Fortunately for me and now for countless others, the brain researchers were beginning to discover that the human brain works in very much the same way as a very powerful computer processor. And we get programmed in much the same way.

The key point here is that I was working with, learning about and programming computers, and at the same time I was reading about how we are a product of our thoughts. At exactly the same time, scientists were unlocking the similarities between computer processing and brain processing—and the timing in my life couldn't have been better.

It all came together for me in 1994, when I ran across a small paperback book by psychologist and researcher Dr. Shad Helmstetter. The title of the book was *What To Say When You Talk To Your Self*. This book helped me to finally figure out how to put into action what I had learned from the verse in Proverbs, and from Earl Nightingale's "Strangest Secret"—that we literally become the product of our thoughts.

Dr. Helmstetter had followed much the same self-education process that I had, when it came to figuring out what makes humans operate the way they do. He also worked personally with Earl Nightingale to develop self-improvement programs, and he learned about the link between computers and the human brain at a time when such information was entirely new.

Then he added the critical piece of information that would

enable us to actually *change*, from the inside out. This third piece of the secret showed me exactly what I needed to do next in order to succeed:

You can reprogram your brain, just like we can reprogram a computer.

If this were true, I thought, if all these experts were right—that the words we say to ourselves, in our own minds, make us into what we are in all areas of our lives—then here was the secret to becoming anything I wanted to be! I finally had a specific, simple way to make lasting changes in my programs, and thereby, in my life.

So I began working with the process of changing what I thought and said to myself and changing my old programs. I read the book, ordered the professionally recorded cassette tape programs that Dr. Helmstetter recommended, and started listening — and the results were nothing short of amazing.

In just a few short years, because I made the decision to actively reprogram my personal mental computer, my life improved in every conceivable way: financially, professionally, and in my relationships with my family and friends. I had learned the real difference between success and failure.

To recap what we've learned so far, here are the three parts of the secret to success that got me where I am today—the same secret that can take you anywhere you want to go in your life:

1. When you program a computer with the wrong information, you get bad results.

2. The human brain acts just like a computer—and we literally live out the results of our programmed thoughts.

3. If you aren't getting the results you want in your life, *you can reprogram yourself for success.*

The nobility of your life as well
as your happiness depends upon the direction
in which that train of thought is going.

—Laurence J. Peter

4

How We Get Programmed for Failure

It has been established by neuroscientists that we carry on a running dialogue in our heads of between 150 and 300 words per minute, which adds up to 45,000 – 51,000 thoughts per day. Most of this chatter is inconsequential ("pick up the dry cleaning", "walk the dog" "I have to go to the bathroom"), but 25 – 30% tends to be negative ("I can't do it", "I'll never pass", "I'm no good at this"), which means we are entertaining 12,000 – 15,000 negative thoughts per day.

During my early work with computers, I learned what we all now know is true: that the keyboard, the mouse, and the microphone are all *input* devices. The resulting commands, carried out by the microprocessor, as a result of a human being typing or clicking or speaking, are known as *output*.

We also know that a human being has several "input" mechanisms for the brain, just as a computer does. Our eyes, ears, and even the nerves in our bodies, all convey vital information to the brain for "processing." And, depending on the sights, sounds or contact with the skin, the brain "outputs" a variety of reactions to the input. That's why the input we got as we were growing up, and continue to get today, is so critically important to our success—or lack of it.

Good input results in good "output" in our lives.
Bad input gives us bad results.

We've established that your brain is like a computer—garbage in, garbage out. You've probably heard that saying many time in your life, and never gave it a second thought.

But I'm asking you to stop right now, put down this book and think about this very carefully: everything you have seen and heard over the years has been processed and stored by your brain—whether that input was positive or negative.

Psychologists tell us that, on the average, by the time they reach the age of 18, young people receive *150,000 negative messages* on what they could not do, or what they could not accomplish. Whether this applies to you, or not, depends on a lot of factors, and may or may not be an exact figure.

But what if it is only half true? What if you have only received 75,000 negative messages in your lifetime, so far? Do you think this might have made a difference in what you believe about yourself, your image of who you are?

What if it was only a quarter of that number—"only" 37,500 negative inputs to your brain? Could this have helped to mold you into the person you are today?

And, would it have made a difference if you could have heard encouraging, uplifting, positive messages about yourself from others as you were growing up?

I was on an airplane the other day and was sitting right behind a woman with a small child about three years old. The little girl had just spilled her drink and the mother was scolding her for being so clumsy. She went on telling her daughter what a klutz she was for about a minute. Finally, I heard the little girl say in a very sweet, quiet voice, "I'm just not having a good day." Well, of course she wasn't! Not as long as her mother was telling her how clumsy she was.

Your brain needs to hear a lot of positive messages to overcome all the negative messages you, and others, have fed it over the years. And, boy, did I have a lot of negative input from my father that I needed to overcome! The fact that he told me I would never be any better, financially, or otherwise, than he had been, was something that I had to completely *erase* from my thinking before I would be able to better myself.

Our parents didn't know any better.

As I mentioned earlier, I had learned over the years that in order to succeed at anything, you must first take control of the powerful mechanism of the brain, and program it to take you in the direction you want to go.

But most parents, especially in the era in which I was raised, didn't know about this. So with the best of intentions, they repeatedly told us all the wrong things about ourselves, our potential, and our ability to succeed.

For example, if a young girl is told by her mother, enough times, that she's "not smart enough to go to college," the girl's brain will process this message and cause her to begin to act in line with that message. Her brain, if it hears this message on a regular basis—despite what the girl's real intelligence or abilities happen to be—will cause her to begin to self-fulfill those negative inputs from her mother.

Imagine what happens to the brain of a 15-year-old boy who is told over and over by his father, "You'll never amount to anything. You're lazy, just like your Uncle Joe, and you'll probably end up in prison by the time you're 18, just like he did!" If the boy hears this enough times, his brain will begin to accept this as fact, and will begin to organize and plan as if prison is the inevitable outcome.

Most of the time, of course, this self-defeating process is unintentional—and many times, unconscious. The human brain is an amazing creation, and is far more powerful in fulfilling our fears or shortcomings than we could ever imagine.

This is the part of your brain that, despite being in an air-conditioned auditorium, with 300 other people around you eating popcorn and drinking a soft drink, causes you to twinge and get nervous when a dinosaur chases a jeep full of people on the screen. You know, intellectually, that the dinosaur cannot harm you—but that primitive part of your brain that acts on the input that it sees and hears, makes the dinosaur *seem* to be capable of harming you—or, at least, the poor actors on the screen.

This also explains why a small child, if told often enough by his parents that he wets the bed because he is a "little baby", will continue to fulfill what he is being programmed to do: in this

case, wet the bed. His brain has no choice. It believes the false
input, and causes him to behave like a little baby—because the
child's brain hears this input constantly from the two humans
it has the most respect for. It trusts their judgment implicitly.
What they say *must be true*, and it doesn't question this input in
the least.

Every input you've ever gotten is still there— and you act out the strongest programs you have.

We know that the brain retains everything it has ever seen
or heard, because scientists have proven it. They have taken
people about to have brain surgery and probed their brains with
small electrical impulses—and those patients have completely
recalled and relived experiences from the past, as if they were
happening all over again, in minute detail. The sights, the
sounds, every emotion was brought back, even though the person experienced those things before the age of three.

The only way those scientists can do that is because it is
all stored there in the brain. And the same exact thing has happened to *you*.

Every word, every experience—every visual, audible or tac-
tile input your brain has received over your lifetime—has been
permanently stored in your subconscious mind. Everything.
It's all stored in there, somewhere.

And, your brain doesn't care if what it sees or hears is actually true or not—it just saves the input. Just as you could type
something on your computer keyboard that isn't true, and your
computer would record the words as faithfully as if they were

true, your brain accepts any input, true or false. It simply stores that input faithfully in your subconscious until it "needs" it to help you process other information or make a decision. Now, this is a scary thought, if you think about it. Your Uncle Jed might say, offhandedly, to you, "Sue, you keep eating like that and you're gonna be just as fat as your Aunt Bessie," and your brain would store that information as if it were 100% true. It would not question it one iota. And, if you heard something along those lines often enough, you would begin to believe it was true, consciously, as well as subconsciously. In effect, your programs end up creating a self-fulfilling prophecy.

That's because the brain always acts on the programs that are the strongest. And, even though Aunt Bessie might tell you not to pay any attention to Uncle Jed, if you heard something like that from him enough times, or something similar from others, your brain would believe, and *act* on, what it heard the most often—the strongest programs.

How did we get to be so negative?

For most people, those 150,000 or so negative messages began with repeated input from your parents or guardians, your siblings, your teachers, and your schoolmates. Then came a whole host of similar negative messages from your associates in life, your fellow workers, advertising, and even the evening news. And if all you have is negative stuff going in, that can put a lot of the wrong kind of programming in place.

Maybe you remember the old saying, "Sticks and stones may break my bones, but words will never hurt me." But try telling that to the child who hears a parent tell him over and over that he is "worthless and will never amount to anything," or that he "has no artistic aptitude," or "can't carry a tune in a bucket."

Those words not only hurt; those words are an outright lie. They cause a child to become something much less than what he or she is capable of becoming. They create wounds that can take a lifetime to heal. They hold us back from being all we could be, and the results can be a lifetime of discouragement and failure.

There is a real good reason why most human beings never reach their true potential and become all that God meant for them to be.

In the next chapter, I will remind some of you of things you heard when you were growing up that may bring back some painful memories.

But it's important that you understand why you have those bad feelings—and what you can do to erase them forever.

For a man's words
will always express
what has been stored
in his heart.

—Luke 6:45

5

Why We Struggle and Fail to Succeed

There could be a very good reason as to why most of us have such a hard time finding success in various areas of our lives.

Think back to your own childhood. Some of the effects of negative verbal input are very likely still operating in your own life. Everything you heard from those you loved or respected (or even your peers) is still lingering in your brain, and may be causing you to be less successful than you could be.

The following list of "words that hurt" may help you recall things your parents said that contributed to shaping your life to this point. See if any of these sound like what was said to you or about you, as you were growing up:

You'll never amount to anything.

Can't you do anything right?

Your room is always a disaster area.

Why can't you be as smart as your sister?

You'll never be smart enough to go to college.

You don't have what it takes to be a doctor.

You are just not musically gifted.

You will turn out to be just like your father.

Are you retarded or something?

Try this: close your eyes and repeat one of the above phrases, with meaning, slowly, 10 times—as if someone else was saying the words to you.

Now, how do you feel? How do you envision yourself? Ask yourself, "Are these words still having an effect on my life? Am I still living out this negative, self-defeating message in my day-to-day activities?"

If this affects you in this way, just imagine what it can do to an impressionable child. Unfortunately, children have not developed the ability to filter out what enters their mental computer. They cannot say, "I accept this compliment, but I reject that criticism." A child views his parents as all-knowing beings whose words are powerful and *true*.

Layer by layer, nearly indelibly, our self-image is created over our lifetime from what we hear and see.

But you know what the sad part is? The sad part is that, in

time, *we ourselves joined in the negative input* and began talking down to ourselves. Inside our brains, we're all talking to ourselves all the time. And, for the vast majority of people, that input is mostly negative.

Bad programming is the answer to the question of why we struggle, fall back, and fail to succeed.

I could give you any number of examples as proof of the disastrous results of this kind of programming.

For instance, in a certain tribe in Africa children are named after the days of the week on which they are born. Half the crimes committed in the village are by those born on Wednesday. Why? Because, in the local language, "Wednesday" also means "violent."

A survey was taken in U.S. prisons which showed that a large percentage of prisoners recalled hearing one or both of their parents repeatedly say to them, "One of these days you are going to end up in jail."

If it is true, as all of those experts claim, that you become what you think about, it makes a lot of sense why we try so hard and still fail.

Is it any wonder why most people are not more successful in life; why we have such a hard time overcoming our mental ceilings, when it comes to financial matters; why we struggle with our relationships, or why we don't seem to be able to get ahead in school or in our careers?

We've all had too much *garbage*, too many bad programs, dumped into our brains over the years—by ourselves and by everybody else!

Imagine if you had an invisible friend that walked around with you all day, every day, who was constantly whispering negative comments about you in your ear. How would you feel at the end of the day? At the end of the week? Would you keep a "friend" like this around for long?

Well, guess what? You're already doing this to *yourself*—and in a far more effective manner than this invisible friend would do it. This is true because you could reject what the friend says—or politely tell them to get lost. *But you can't get away from yourself—from your own thoughts and your own old mental programs that limit your picture of you.*

It may be happening right now, as you read.

It's a constant process, one that is going on even as you read this book. You may be saying to yourself something like, "Oh, sure, this one little secret can change my life, sure it can, Patrick. And I suppose this simple secret is all it will take to make me rich and famous? Ha! This sounds like a bunch of new-age hokey pokey to me!"

If that is what you are thinking right now, or something similar, that's just your old negative self-talk running its same tired old script. That script gets you to doubt yourself and every other good thing that comes your way.

And, you're so used to it by now that you probably don't even notice when it happens!

Your negative self-talk happens in the background, without you even knowing it.

This inner dialogue is going on all the time—but most of it is going on "below the surface," so to speak. That is, it is going on below the conscious threshold, most of the time. It happens without you ever being aware of it.

You could be taking a test, for example, and even though most of your thought processes are concentrated on the question and its answer, your old programs are still running in the background. They are saying things like, "Oh, man, I just know I'm going to flunk this test. I didn't study like I should have, and now it's caught up with me. This will probably make my grade drop, and my dad is going to blow his top. Why couldn't I have been born as smart as that nerd in front of me? I was just born to be a big failure!"

Or, how about the first time you met the "girl of your dreams." You might have had something like this going on in your head: "This is the most exquisite creature I have ever seen. She probably thinks I am a loser. That's because I am. I'm the ugliest guy in the room, and she is the prettiest girl. I don't have a snowball's chance in hell to get her to go out with me. She is probably laughing at me right now for even looking at her from across the room. I'll never find someone like that to be my girl."

This all goes on inside our heads, of course, sometimes in a split-second's time. We have done it so often that it is almost imperceptible and unconscious.

This is why negative programming is so demoralizing and

debilitating. It starts with your parents, teachers and friends. Over time, you, yourself, automatically start adding more self-defeating programs that agree with what is already there. You get so used to doing it and responding to it that you don't consciously pay any attention to it. You are, in effect, giving yourself very powerful, almost hypnotic suggestions to feel bad and to perform poorly.

If you're less successful in any area of your life today than you want to be, I can guarantee you that part of the fault lies with the input you've gotten along the way. It's just like that program I was writing for the FDA—Garbage In, Garbage Out.

If you're failing, it's because you were programmed to fail.

But that doesn't mean it has to stay that way.

In the following chapters, we'll go over specific, simple steps you can take, starting right now, to begin "erasing and replacing" the old programs with new ones that work best for you. Along the way, I'll share with you the success stories of people just like you who have changed their self-talk for the better, and who are enjoying the results every day.

You'll want to keep a notebook handy to jot down your thoughts, ideas and "aha's" as you go. It's time to change some of your old negative programs. We're going to start that process by taking a look at what the negative programs actually look like, so you can recognize them when they show up.

Our mind can shape the way a thing will be,
because we act according to our expectations.

—Federico Fellini

6

How To Identify the Old Programming

In order for you to get from where you are now in your life to where you want to go, we first need to take a look at some examples of what your old negative programs look like. Once you know how to identify the programs you'd be better off without, you can continue with the process of getting rid of them by replacing them with something better.

There are several "clues" as to whether or not if you have been programmed in the wrong way. See if any of these show up in your own life.

One way to know if you have some faulty programming is if you focus only on problems, instead of solutions, throughout the day. This is the mindset of failure, to see first what won't work instead of what will.

You've heard the old saying, "The glass is either half-full or it is half-empty, depending on your point of view." Well, it's true, and if you tend to see the situations in your life as "Oh, woe is me, this is a disaster," this is a clue you are in the wrong state of mind and need some re-programming.

Secondly, perhaps you tend to stereotype other people. By putting others, and ourselves, into preconceived "pigeon-holes," we avoid thinking of people as unique, worthy individuals. This leads to strained relationships and gives us an undeserved sense of superiority or inferiority, as we all tend to compare ourselves with others more than we should. This could be another clue that you are saying some things to yourself that are self-defeating.

Next, ask yourself if you tend to think in absolutes. If so, you may tend to program yourself negatively. For example, if you exaggerate reality with words like "always," "never," and "everyone," as in "I always drop thing – I am such a klutz," this indicates you have a mindset that is tuned pessimistically.

When you think only in extremes of all or nothing, you distort reality. Your efforts become total failures or complete successes—with nothing in between.

Another clue: do you always expect the worst, thinking such things as, "What if I don't get the job?" and "What if I fail the exam?" Expecting the worst does not encourage you to behave effectively. Expecting the worst only promotes anxiety and negative input to your brain.

Here's another hint that you may have had some bad programming: if you tend to assign negative labels to other people all the time. Labels are the tools we use to lower self-esteem in ourselves and others. Examples of this kind of labeling would be: "I'm so stupid" or "I'm such a fat slob" or "You are such a loser."

When we say phrases like these often, they become a part

of our identity, and we begin to believe what we are saying about ourselves or someone else.

For some people, everything is a catastrophe.

Here's another indication of bad programming going on in your head: every bad thing that happens is a horrible disaster, the end of the world. This is an easy habit for any of us to fall into, being a "drama queen" about everything that happens to us or to others. We all know it's better to lighten up and look at the glass as half full once in a while—but with the wrong programs, we often only see our limitations.

And what about this bad habit: do you find yourself always blaming others? Oftentimes, we tend to assign guilt, instead of solving the problem. If we can blame others, we feel vindicated in a situation and can avoid taking personal responsibility for the results of our own actions. Again, this is the result of bad programming, either from others or, more likely, from ourselves.

Another clue: do you hear yourself saying, "Yes, but . . . " a lot? When someone offers a possible solution to your problem, do you start out with "Yes, but . . ." and then list reasons why the proposed solution won't work? "Yes, but . . . " says "I'm really not listening to you right now—I've already made up my mind, the vote is in and my old programs of doubt are in first place, no matter what you say next!"

When someone else suggests a solution, a person with more positive programs would likely say something like, "That is a terrific idea!"

There is still room to address the potential drawbacks of the idea, without being automatically negative from the beginning.

Another result of bad programming is over-generalizing and jumping to false conclusions. This is similar to stereotyping other people and thinking in absolutes. It means that the wrong programs can cause us to take a single instance or occurrence, and generalize it to numerous other situations—even when the logic doesn't hold up. For example: "Bill is a nice man, and he doesn't want to date me. Therefore, no nice man will ever want to date me."

To assume something like this looks silly when you see it in the clear light of day—but we do it to ourselves all the time. To prove this, all you have to do is listen to the things people say out loud, about themselves and their own ability to succeed— or *not*.

See if you've heard any of the following phrases lately, or even said them yourself.

"I can never remember people's names."

Most people are guilty of saying this at one time or another. You know what happens when you go into a party, you meet somebody for the first time, and there's a huge crowd of people. You shake that first person's hand, looking around and saying to yourself, "I'll never remember this guy's name!"

An hour later when you see that person again, guess what? Your brain is proud of itself! You told it you couldn't remember his name, and so, sure enough, your brain immediately forgot it!

How about this one:

"Oh, brother, it's going to be another one of those days."

Ever heard anybody say that at work? Try this. Go up to somebody at work and just look right at them and say, "Ernest, you know, you're just not looking real good today. You look a little sickly. Are you sure you feel all right?" Fifteen minutes later, send somebody else over to say the same thing—and then, an hour later, have someone else say something along the same lines.

By noon, poor Ernest will be at home! He'll be sicker than a dog. He'll believe it. You know why? Repetition. His brain had no choice. It begins to believe what it hears over and over again.

What about this one:

"I am so clumsy."   ا حُرَف
غير مُنقّف

I heard a waitress say that the other day. She dropped something and immediately mumbled "Oh, I'm so clumsy," as she picked it up—probably just an attempt to ease the embarrassment of the moment.

Then, a little while later, in another part of the restaurant, I heard something else drop. And guess what I heard right after that? "Oh, I'm so clumsy." I bet that waitress drops things all day long! You see, her brain has been programmed to believe it, simply from saying that to herself over and over again every day.

How about this one:

"It seems like I'm always broke."

Folks, if you say that kind of thing to yourself enough times, guess what you're telling your brain? "I'm going to stay right where I am, financially." And you will! I know, because I said things like that to myself for the first 45 years of my life.

Then, one day, I remember taking a walk with my wife. We had walked a couple of blocks without saying anything, because we had been arguing earlier about my career situation and our lack of money to pay bills. We were using the answering machine to screen out the bill collectors, and this was causing her some stress, as you can imagine. Besides, we wanted to do some of the things in life that it takes money to do—like travel—before we got too old to enjoy it.

I had just finished reading another book on self-talk, and I had begun to reprogram my brain concerning money. So, I said to Linda, "Honey, we've lived the first half of our lives struggling, financially. Well, I'm tired of it, and I know you are, so, beginning today, we're going to live the second half of our lives rich!"

I know she didn't believe me, bless her heart, because all she said was, "That would be nice." But I knew it would be true, because I now knew "the secret" and how to apply it. And the positive results of that decision, to reprogram my brain concerning money, have been prevalent in my life ever since.

Here's another example of a common negative program you might recognize:

"I always freeze up in front of a group."

Have you ever said something like that, when you were asked to give a presentation or speech? Did you know that public speaking is America's number 1 fear, and death is the number 2 fear? That means that most people in America are actually more afraid of speaking in public than they are of dying.

Think about it—that means that at funerals, most people would rather be in the coffin than standing up front giving the eulogy!

If I were to write them all down, the list of common negative programs would go on for pages. However, even if I did, I would only be scratching the surface of the thousands of self-defeating programs we give ourselves every day.

I'll include just a few more here. Is there any chance you've heard yourself say any of these things lately?

I'll probably catch a cold now.

I just can't seem to get organized.

I'm not any good at sales.

Everything I touch turns to manure!

That's just my luck.

Sometimes I just hate myself.

I don't have the energy I used to.

I'm really out of shape.

I never win anything.

I feel like I'm over the hill.

I never have any money left at the end of the month.

I lose weight but then I gain it right back again.

I get so depressed!

I'll never get it right!

Ok, maybe you don't say or think these kinds of things—but do any of these phrases sound like something you hear *other people* say? Are you convinced yet that you—or at least someone you know—might just have a problem with this "negative mind programming"?

In the next chapter, I'm going to show you why many of the things you've tried in the past didn't work, or why the positive changes didn't last—and what you can do about it.

Our belief at the beginning
of a doubtful undertaking
is the one thing that ensures
the successful outcome
of our ventures.

—William James

7

Why the Best of Self-Help
Can Still Fail

If you're reading this, there's a pretty good chance that you've tried before to get past your roadblocks to success. There's also a good chance that you've tried one or more things in the past that either didn't work at all, or worked for awhile and then stopped working.

That's because your old programs of negativity and self-doubt were still in the way. For instance, what if you have all the desire in the world to change your life, but deep down, you don't really believe you *deserve* to succeed?

You may be where you are right now in your life because you've been programmed to think you didn't deserve any better. That's what happened to me, and it held me back for many years.

As I mentioned in the preface, just a few short years ago we lived in a small house in the north part of Fort Worth. I had been in the same home, a tiny little cookie-cutter house in a middle-class suburban development for 17 years.

I had two old cars that were 'clunkers' that we could barely keep running; they were literally falling apart all the time. One of them seemed to run on pure oil—no gasoline, I had to pour a quart of oil straight through it every day!

We had several major credit cards, all maxed out. And you already know that, yes, I've used my answering machine to screen out the bill collectors. I'm telling you all this because that was my background; that's where I had come from.

You know why? My dad left when I was 12 years old; I never saw him again. He left town with another woman and we never got any money out of him: no alimony money, no support money, nothing whatsoever. And back then, they just didn't have "good lawyers" like they have nowadays to help with a situation like that.

My mom had to work two and sometimes three jobs just to put food on the table. I worked, like I said, since I was 14 years old, and grew up in the poorest part of Fort Worth.

A "legacy" that limited me for years ...

I'm telling you these things only for this reason: I believe I now know why I was in the negative mental state that I was until I was 45 years old. The reason I was in that mental state is because my dad made it clear when he was there that my brothers and I would never amount to anything. He let us know that we would never get beyond his level of income, his social status in life. In today's dollars, he never made more than about

$15,000 a year in his whole lifetime. He jumped from job to job, never being successful at anything he did.

He let us know, clearly and unmistakably, in many different ways, that, socially and economically, you never rise above your parents' status in life.

So mentally, that's what I thought was the reality for me. I was convinced of that because my father had said this to me over the years in so many ways. That's how my brain had repeatedly been "programmed" for failure.

Oh, I tried to change my outlook on life many times. I bought every "self-help" book there was. You're familiar with those self-help books, aren't you? You've seen those books on *How to Lose Friends and Alienate People*, and others along that line? The bookstore shelves are full of them and it seems like I'd read them all. I spent hundreds of dollars on them building quite a collection.

And, in fact, some of the things in those books are pretty good. You've probably read things like:

believe in yourself

keep your priorities straight

take responsibility for yourself

Wouldn't you agree that if you could do all of those things in all of those books, you'd be a better person, and you'd be more successful in life? I mean, really, if you could just:

think big

control your stress

be aggressive and assertive

visualize the outcome

... and you could apply all those principles in your life, surely you would be more successful in all areas of your life, right? All those things are good, sound principles, aren't they? How about these:

set specific goals

work hard

believe money is good

manage your time

dress for success

learn to sell yourself

take time off

stay motivated

meditate

be optimistic

pay attention to details

get organized

don't procrastinate

stay in control

see problems as opportunities

The list goes on and on. And they're all good things to practice in our lives.

Well, you can save your money on buying all those self-help books. I just summarized for you everything that you'll ever read in just about any self-help book out there!

The problem is, these principles do not work the way your human brain does.

Look, you can read a book and three months from now when you walk by the bookshelf, the book doesn't call out to you and say, "Hey, do you remember this principle? Have you forgotten you should be dressing for success, you slob?" It doesn't do that, right?

It would be nice if we could be reminded of all those good principles, automatically, from day to day, but it just doesn't work that way. Hey, you might even forget something I've shared in this book someday!

Motivational Rallies Won't Help Much After The First Day

You've probably been to one of those one-day motivational rallies where a series of speakers gets up to "pump you up," tell you how to think positive, and all sorts of other ideas along those lines. You know, for only fifty dollars you can get pumped up and motivated . . . at least for a day!

Then, what happens after that one day of motivation? What happens to the motivation then? Well, for one thing, it's in those cassette tapes that they sold at the back of the room that you decided not to spend more money on!

You see, to really get anything good out of those pep-rallies, you'd have to continue to motivate yourself, over and over again. That's because these principles don't stick. Your brain doesn't remember them after only reading or hearing them one time. Again, that's just not the way your brain works.

In order to create permanent, lasting change, you've got to use a solution that works the way the human brain is designed to work in the first place. And the most powerful aspect of the programming process, the one that makes real change possible, is the power of repetition. Let me repeat that: The one aspect of the process that makes real change possible, is the power of *repetition.*

And as you will see, repetition is the key to learning anything – even the wrong things.

The one thing over which
you have absolute control
is your own thoughts.
It is this that puts you in a position
to control your own destiny.

—Paul G. Thomas

8

The Power of Repetition

Just how does the brain actually learn and <u>retain</u> ideas and concepts? First of all, do you know that your brain believes everything that it sees and hears . . . enough times? It's the repetition that creates those strong programs. Let me prove that to you.

During the Vietnam War, there were very <u>patriotic</u> American men who became Communists. In just a few short months of captivity as Prisoners of War, they began to believe that all they had heard about America was false. They believed that the free enterprise system was not what we said it was and that democracy was not the way of life that they should believe in and live in and promote. They became Communists. Do you know how?

It's called brainwashing. And it works.

Do you know how they reprogrammed those men's minds? It was simple. They would put them in small prison cells and blast recorded lies about the American way of life, over and over and over, night and day, for weeks on end.

And, slowly, but surely, many of these patriotic American soldiers began to believe all those lies—because they heard it enough times. See, I told you that was the secret to the whole learning process: simple repetition.

Remember, when the brain hears something, it doesn't matter whether it is true or not. Your brain will accept as truth the input it receives, if it hears it enough times, from a credible source. (In the case of the Prisoners of War, they used voices that sounded like the President, movie stars and other famous Americans to make the lies more "credible.")

Why Young People Join Gangs and Cults

This is exactly what happens to someone who is subjected to faulty input. Given enough time, inundated with enough data, enough false input, almost anyone can be convinced of almost anything, whether based on fact or fiction.

This is why young people join street gangs and religious cults. Whether a person is young or old, smart or dumb, educated or uneducated—it doesn't matter.

Deluge them with enough distorted data, over a long period of time, and they can have their views, their realities, and their values completely altered.

Patricia Hearst is the heiress to the Hearst fortune. In 1974, she was kidnapped by a radical terrorist group called the Symbionese Liberation Army. This incident was one of the strangest kidnapping cases that the F.B.I. has ever been involved in. Not only did it result in one of the largest manhunts of all time but it also helped to prove that kidnapping had disastrous effects on the person that was kidnapped.

While under control of the S.L.A., Patricia Hearst was forced to rob a bank and protect her S.L.A. "comrades." She was brainwashed, which included spending over 50 days in a closet. When found, she was put on trial for grand theft, and was convicted. She spent almost two years of a seven year term, and was released with help from President Jimmy Carter.

Scary, isn't it?

Here's what's really scary: your own self-concept has very likely been based, at least to some degree, on this type of distorted thinking.

You, too, may be getting "brainwashed", in a way that is just as harmful as getting sucked into a socio-political or religious cult.

The most powerful brainwasher you will ever encounter is *you*.

That's good news, though—because that means if the programming process is so powerful and effective in the negative, it can also be used to install positive programs just as strongly.

One of the most obvious ways we've all been programmed is through the use of repetition in advertising. Let's have some fun by seeing what your brain can recall; what you might not even *realize* it has stored within it.

To Prove My Point . . . An Advertising Quiz

I can prove to you how powerful repetition really is. I am going to list some advertising slogans that you have probably heard at one time or another in the past. See how many products you can identify with these slogans:

SLOGANS

Double your pleasure, double your fun . . .

Good to the last drop.

I'd walk a mile for a _____.

Nothin' says lovin' like somethin' from the oven!

Betcha can't eat just one.

Finger-lickin' good.

I can't believe I ate the whole thing!

Quality is job 1.

Please don't squeeze the _____.

The pause that refreshes.

You're in good hands with _____.

When you say _____, you've said it all.

Nothing comes between me and my _____.

Where's the beef?

Fly the friendly skies.

Does she, or doesn't she?

How do you spell relief?

The best part of waking up, is _____ in your cup.

You'll wonder where the yellow went, when you brush your teeth with _____.

Reach out and touch someone.

You deserve a break today.

THE POWER OF REPETITION

Have it your way.

Be all that you can be.

I've got a headache this big and it's got ____ written all over it.

You can trust your car to the man who wears the star.

Melts in your mouth, not in your hand.

See the USA, in a _____.

You've come a long way, baby!

We're number two…we try harder.

Wouldn't you really rather have a _____?

PRODUCTS

Wrigley's Doublemint gum

Maxwell House coffee

Camel cigarettes

Pillsbury poppin' fresh pastries

Lay's potato chips

Kentucky Fried Chicken

Alka-Seltzer

Ford automobiles

Charmin toilet paper

Coca-Cola

Allstate insurance

Budweiser beer

Calvin's (jeans)

Wendy's

United Airlines

Clairol hair coloring

Rolaids antacid

Folger's coffee

Pepsodent toothpaste

AT&T long distance

McDonald's

Burger King

The US Army

Excedrin

Texaco

M&Ms

Chevrolet

Virginia Slims cigarettes

Avis

Buick

If you got fewer than 15 right, you're probably in your 20's or younger. If you got between 16 and 25 correct, you're pretty normal.

And if by any chance you got 30 out of 30, you've got a great memory—and you seriously need to get a life!

Now, think about this. Advertising companies don't spend millions of dollars to "program our minds" with this stuff if repetition doesn't work. Do you know that some of these phrases haven't been heard or used for over 30 years? Why did your brain recall a lot of them? Because of repetition. You heard it enough times, over and over again, on TV or the radio, and *your brain just could not forget it.*

Repetition is the Key

So, here's one of the keys to this whole reprogramming process: *repetition*. That's all there is to it. The key to success in reprogramming your brain with the new, positive, image-building self-talk is the same way it was programmed with the bad stuff in the first place: through repetition.

If you listen to the good input enough times, your brain simply does not have a choice. It will begin to think the good thoughts that will eventually lead to the good things in your life. You still need to set the right goals and have a game plan to get where you want to go; but once you change your programs, all those other good self-help concepts will suddenly be much more effective for you.

Don't just put this book aside, thinking it is just too simple. B*ecause* it is so simple this should excite you and motivate you to start reprogramming your brain, starting today.

Now, play along with me just for a moment...

Just ask yourself "what if." Take a moment and say to yourself, "What if this simple secret that Patrick is sharing with me could help make me into the person I've always wanted to be? What if it could help me lose the weight I've always wanted to lose? What if it could change my relationships with other people, to positive, loving relationships? What if it could change my attitude towards money and allow me to begin to have more of it in my life?"

Would it be worth your time if all these things could come to pass by simply changing your self-talk?

As one of my assignments in an English class in college, I read a small book by a man named James Allen entitled *As A Man Thinketh*. This passage jumped out at me as I read:

The aphorism, "As a man thinketh in his heart, so is he," not only embraces the whole of a man's being, but is so comprehensive as to reach out to every condition and circumstance of his life.
A man is literally what he thinks, his character being the complete sum of all his thoughts.
As the plant springs from, and could not be without the seed, so every act of man springs from the hidden seeds of thought, and could not have appeared without them.

Now, if this is true, here is the secret to having or becoming anything you want; the secret to changing anything about yourself that you don't like:

to change your thoughts, you simply need to change the words that go into your brain

—and repeat the new self-talk often enough so that it becomes your new "autopilot" program.

Think about it. If everything you are is a result of what you have had "input" into your brain since birth, then doesn't it make sense that if you change the input, you will change your life?

I'm living proof that this process works. And, if your input had been just a little different as you were growing up, would you have been a different person? Would you be doing the same thing for a living? Would you be who you are today?

Speak the affirmative;
emphasize your choice
by utterly ignoring
all that you reject.

—**Emerson**

9

What If Your Input Had Been Different?

In a study conducted by a leading Midwestern university, graduate students followed 2-year-old children around and recorded every time their parents said something positive to them, and every time they said something negative. The results were startling! On average, the children heard 432 negative and 32 positive statements per day—a ratio of *fourteen to one!*

Negative beliefs gained in early years are carried over into later life. In a study conducted at UCLA, incoming freshmen were asked to list their personal strengths and weaknesses. Now, remember, these were bright young students at one of the best universities in California, yet on average, their lists of weaknesses were *six times longer* than their lists of strengths.

If you're like most people, you're burdened with a self-image that isn't as good as it could be.

Think about this: How many times do you remember receiving positive, uplifting, edifying, good input from your parents and your siblings, as you grew up? It happens so rarely for some folks that they can count the number of positive inputs on one hand.

I even get a little emotional writing about this, because I really didn't have that kind of positive input from my parents—not like I could have had. And I certainly don't blame them; they probably didn't have the positive input they needed from their parents either.

It's worth changing your programs just for your own sake. But it matters even more if you're a parent yourself. If you have children of your own, the question now is, *are you willing to break this self-defeating cycle?*

Would Positive Input Have Made A Difference?

What if your programming had been different as you grew up? What if you had heard things like this: "Honey, you're the best (painter, singer, drum player, speller, whatever) in the whole world!"

What if you had heard that, every day, from somebody you really loved and trusted all your life?

Or what if you had heard something like, "I believe you can do whatever you set your mind to do." What if you had heard that over and over and over as you grew up?

"It seems like you get better at that every time you do it."

"I'm so proud of you and your determination to succeed at this!"

"I've never seen anyone with a more positive outlook on life."

Folks, if you had gotten that kind of input, instead of the kind that most of us got, do you think you'd be a different person? Would you be doing the same thing for a living? Would you be married to the same person? Would you live in the same neighborhood? Would you be making the same amount of money?

I don't know, but my guess is that with the right kind of programming, your own children could be the kind of human successes that you'd like to be—and it's not too late for you, either.

Are Other People Just "Luckier"?

Do you think other people are just luckier than you are? Do you really think that's true—or perhaps did they just get better programming than you did?

You see people with lots of nice things, and maybe you think of that person as successful, but maybe they just had different programming from their folks and their friends and relatives.

Maybe they learned how to replace the old programs with the new ones, like I learned how to do a few years ago.

Just imagine what you could do and be if you could override all the old programs and replace them with brand new, positive, uplifting thoughts and encouraging words.

Think about how you think now about money and success. If you could erase all of the old programming and put in new, would it make a difference in your outlook on life?

Think how much more enthusiasm for life you would have, and how much more you could accomplish, if all the shackles were suddenly gone. Do you know what shackles I'm talking about? Some of you don't even realize you have those shackles on.

I'm talking about the shackles of self-doubt.

You may be doubting right now, for example, whether or not you can be as successful as someone else you know.

Or you may be wondering whether or not this book can really help you.

You see, those shackles have kept you back in a lot of different areas of life. And they may be holding you back even as you read this book.

I read an "Archie" comic strip back when I was a teenager, and it had a lighthearted jab at positive thinking that points out this tendency to doubt our ability to better ourselves.

As I recall it, Jughead tells Archie he fears he will fail at something he wants to do. Archie then gives Jughead this advice: "Tell yourself you can do it! Speak positive messages of success to yourself!"

Jughead answers, "That won't work. I know what a liar I am!"

It's funny when it's about a character in a comic book, but it gets serious when it comes to your own life and creating the future you want.

For now, it's okay if your brain doesn't quite believe the

power of this solution yet. For the moment, just consider this.

What if there is a way?

What if there is a way to get rid of the old programming completely? Would it free you up to become the person you know inside you deserve to be?

I didn't believe the new programs at first either, until they became stronger than my old programmed beliefs of self-doubt.

But I kept going in spite of my natural skepticism—and because I did, today my wife and I live a life that, before, we could only dream of.

If you want to make the kind of changes in your life that will lead to true, lasting success, let me encourage you. It's not only possible, it's easy—and it works whether you believe in it at first, or not.

In order to defeat the old negative programs, you have to "write over them" with newer, more positive programs. In the next chapter, I'm going to tell you exactly how to do that.

You are today where your thoughts have brought you;
you will be tomorrow where your thoughts take you.

—James Lane Allen

10

How To Replace Your Old Programs

That negative programming of your brain that I've been talking about has to be erased and replaced, or it will continue to direct everything you do for the rest of your life. In order to make permanent, lasting changes, you must learn how to reprogram your brain—and I'm going to teach you how to do it yourself.

Wouldn't it be something if, somehow, that secret I learned just a few short years ago could help you literally reprogram yourself for success? If it worked, do you think it would change your life for the better?

If you look at the References at the end of this book, you will find that this information is no longer really a secret at all. This concept of positive self-talk, (some call this "affirmations,") has been taught by leading psychologists for decades. But for most people, it *is* still a secret—or, at least, most people don't recognize the incredible life-changing power there is to be found by using it. My desire, with this book, is to spread the word, far and wide, so more people can benefit from using these self-talk reprogramming techniques.

Author Adam Khan shares a story in his book *Self Help Stuff That Works* about how Randall Masciana, M.S., found out what kind of mental strategy most improved a person's performance when throwing darts. Masciana asked his dart-players to try everything from mental imagery (visualizing hitting the target) to Zen meditation (clearing the mind of extraneous thoughts).

Masciana discovered that positive self-talk was the best technique for improving the dart thrower's ability to hit the target. Simply by talking to oneself in a confident, reassuring, positive, friendly way, the ability to throw darts improved drastically!

Now if positive self-talk can help someone play the game of darts better, what could it do for someone who was determined to play the game of life better?

So, how do you get rid of the garbage? How do you erase your old programming and replace it with new programs—programs that can make you into the success you have always dreamed of being, and that you are fully capable of becoming, in every area of your life?

We all could use a little magic.

If only there were a magic wand that we could wave that would cause all the old, negative, self-defeating programming to be erased—and that, with another wave, could replace the old input with new, uplifting, encouraging, positive, motivating input!

What you say to yourself, in your mind, in your thoughts, on a daily basis—your own self-talk—is that magic wand. Remember, in spite of all the negative things you might say out loud, the most powerful self-talk is usually not actual verbalized words coming from your mouth, but the dialogue that constantly goes on inside your head—inside your mind.

The words your brain "hears," whether audibly or inaudibly, are the keys to changing your input from negative to positive, from self-defeating to self-fulfilling.

In order to change your old programs by replacing them with something better, all you need is the script of words you need to say to yourself, and a way to hear the words of the message, repeatedly, without much effort required on your part. If it's too difficult, we stop doing it—and that's why self-talk reprogramming is so simple.

ʃ Ok, here's the solution to our bad programming dilemma. Our brains are full of the negative programming and we have to change the input, the actual words that we hear, and we have to replace the old programming with new.

Remember, whatever this secret "tool" is that I'm about to share with you, it has to be simple, permanent, and has to give you the new word-for-word set of directions, the new programming, the actual words for success. And, it has to be based on the way the brain works.

The only solution that I know of that we've come up with in the past 30 years that can change our mindset in that way, is positive, upbeat, encouraging self-talk.

I told you that you were talking to yourself all the time. One way or the other you are saying things to yourself, in your head, constantly.

And, by the way, it's not so bad when you talk to yourself. It's not even bad when you answer yourself. As Zig Ziglar says, it's when you talk to yourself—and then answer yourself—and then you say, "Huh?" When that happens, then you know there is a problem!

The Magic Reprogramming Tool

As it turns out, there *is* a small "magic tool" that can help you with this reprogramming. It was invented several years ago, and it can help you change your life. To start with, it was a little device called the cassette recorder—but these days, the new self-talk programs come on CD. There are many self-talk CD subjects available on the market today (see Resources), to address all your reprogramming areas.

This simple little tool will allow you to listen to the new words, the actual positive programming that your brain needs to hear, over and over and over, effortlessly. It can provide that automatic repetition that we talked about earlier, which is so important.

Listen as you sleep, as you work, as you drive, as you relax. Anytime, day or night, while you're doing something else. The listening is actually more effective if you don't focus on it, than if you do.

Here is just one example (from Dr. Shad Helmstetter's book, *The Self-Talk Solution*) of the type of thing you can expect to hear recorded on a professional self-talk CD:

"Today, I have a choice. I can say and think positive, uplifting things to and about myself, or I can do the opposite. I choose to purposely and actively input the good thoughts and verbalize them to myself constantly throughout the day. Today is going to be one of the most productive, upbeat experiences of my life. I am going to make the most of every situation, no matter how challenging it might be. Challenges only force me to grow and expand my patience, compassion, and love for others."

Friend, you can't listen to this kind of stuff over and over again without changing your life!

Just remember, it takes lots of repetition. Remember those 150,000 negative inputs I told you most people receive before they are adults? You've got to listen to the new programming a lot to overcome all that garbage!

Just play the CDs as often as you can—as you get ready for work in the morning, as you fall asleep at night, as you drive to and from work. Play them "in the background", if you wish. No matter how loud the volume, as long as your ears hear the words repeatedly, they will do the job of reprogramming your brain, slowly but surely.

How I Lost 15 Pounds Without Trying

Now let me tell you how I know that this works. When I first got into this, I needed to lose some weight. I needed to lose about 15 pounds at the time, and so I listened to some tapes I had recorded on how to lose weight. As recently as a few years ago, we didn't know yet that it worked better to listen to a professional voice than your own—since we hear all our own imperfections in the recording when we make it ourselves. But the home-made tapes were scripted right and I made sure the recording quality was good.

As I was getting ready for work every morning I would listen to a tape to change my old programs about weight, health and fitness in general.

The first month, listening to positive words concerning hunger, my eating habits, exercise and health in general, I lost about 4 or 5 pounds. It wasn't much, but it was a lot for me because I didn't purposely, consciously change anything about my exercise routine or my diet. I just listened to the words that helped me to think differently about eating and exercise and all the things that help you to lose weight—and that initial success gave me the motivation to continue until I reached my 15-pound goal.

The repetition is what does it. The tapes or CDs, can be played in the background so that it doesn't even have to be conscious. As long as you can physically hear the recorded new messages of self-belief, they will do their job of reprogramming you for success.

How My Daughter Stopped Biting Her Nails

Let me give you another example, from my own family's experience.

My daughter was 13 when I started listening to these tapes. I was listening to self-help tapes everywhere we drove in a car, all around the house—I had tapes playing all the time.

One day she came to me and said, "Dad, I've been biting my nails too much, and I have tried to stop, but I can't." She would bite them right down to the nub; it was terrible.

My wife had tried putting hot sauce on them to solve the problem. Have you ever heard of that? You put this clear hot sauce on there so that when they bite their nails the taste of the hot sauce makes your mouth burn.

But, living in Texas, we had taken our daughter to Mexican restaurants since she was two years old and it didn't work, because she loves hot sauce!

So, in desperation, she came to me and said, "Dad, I hear all those tapes you listen to all the time. Do you think there is something you could come up with to help me?" I said, "Well, let me see what I can do."

I recorded a little 10-minute tape and bought one of those tape recorders at Radio Shack that plays the tape in one direction and then reverses and plays it in the opposite direction. We ran a little pillow speaker from the tape recorder to under her pillow, and she listened to that message all night long for 30 days.

She came to me towards the end of the first month and showed me her beautiful nails. She had not bitten them at all. In fact, she was even surprised. She said, "Dad, how does this stuff work? I don't understand it. I don't consciously remember doing anything different." I said, "Honey, your brain didn't have a choice."

It really didn't, you know. And the same thing is true for you. If it hears the positive input enough, your brain has no other choice but to program in, and eventually believe, the strong new information that tells the positive truth about you, in advance. Isn't that exciting? What if you could apply this to any area of your life that needed improvement?

You can. And when it comes to being successful in our lives, the biggest area most people focus on is the area of money and finances.

Why you may not be wealthy . . . yet.

Many (or most) of us have been programmed for failure, when it comes to wealth and financial freedom. Let's see if you have some negative thoughts about money.

Do you think money is the cause of all evil, you know, the root of all evil? Well, it's not. In fact, money is a very valuable tool in bringing about good in the world. Now the *love of money* is something different, because it's not when you get the money, it's when the money gets you—that's when you're in trouble. The moment the money begins to control you, and the moment you depend on money for your happiness—in my opinion, that's when you have the wrong emphasis in your life.

The sad part is, we have *all* been programmed to think of money in a negative way, at least to some extent.

Let me prove it to you. Have you ever driven through one of those real nice, fancy neighborhoods? I'm talking about the multi-million dollar homes—the kind you've only dreamed of living in. You're in a different world, you know? So, you're driving through one of these high-class neighborhoods with these big, fancy homes and you look at them, and then, you look at your spouse and say something along these lines:

"Crooks. Honey, all these folks have got to be crooks! You

can't make this kind of money legally! They're all into drugs or prostitution or some other shady stuff. That's the only way you could possibly make this kind of dough!"

Now if you've never even *thought* that kind of thing, then maybe you don't have negative thoughts about money. But most people can relate to that statement; they've thought that, or something similar, at least once in their lives.

Do you know why? Because the media teaches us that it's evil to have money. Who are the people who have money on TV and in the movies? The bad guys, the pimps, the prostitutes, and the politicians, right?

So, you've more than likely been programmed negatively and need new programming regarding wealth. Otherwise, you will continue to believe the negative programming about money, and you will not do what it takes to generate more wealth.

The truth about your money programs.

People who are wealthy think it's all right to have lots of money. People who are poor think money will never be plentiful in their life. Both are correct! The truth is, when it comes to having and making money, you'll be exactly as successful as your programs allow you to be. And the same is true for anything else in your life at which you want to be more successful.

If you'd like to see what the new, successful self-talk programs should sound like when it comes to money and financial freedom, look in the Appendix for specific scripts like the ones you'll hear on the self-talk CDs on this subject. There are professionally recorded programs to help you become more successful in every area of your life.

For example, imagine listening to this kind of statement each day:

"I see money as a positive and powerful tool with which I'm able to accomplish many good and worthwhile things in my life and in the lives of others."

Now, friend, you say that enough times and, believe me, in 30 days or so your brain will begin to actually believe that it's true, that money is just a tool. And, as you continue, your brain will help you figure out how to get more money, so you can use it to accomplish those good and worthwhile things in the lives of others.

Did you know that money is just a measure of your service to others? That's all it is. Have you served enough people yet? If you don't have the money that you'd like to have, maybe you haven't served enough people in life. Give people what they want or find a need and fill it, and the money will come as a result.

If you want to be more successful when it comes to money, it's perfectly fine to start by working on your old programs specifically about that. But bear in mind, when you start listening to the professional self-talk, the improvements from that listening area will spill over into other areas of your life as well.

In the next chapter, I'm going to share with you some real-life examples of how positive self-talk has changed people's lives. And as you'll hear, the same impact holds true whether you're someone famous, or more "ordinary." The most exciting part of all is that your own success in any and every area of your life is limited only by your belief in yourself, and your willingness to try.

In the next chapter, I will share with you stories of others who have reprogrammed themselves for success, using self-talk.

The thing always happens
that you really believe in;
and the belief in a thing
makes it happen.

—**Frank Lloyd Wright**

11

Does This Reprogramming Really Work?

In one of their *Chicken Soup for the Soul* books, Mark Victor Hansen and Jack Canfield tell a story that is the ultimate example of positive self-talk.

A little boy is alone in the yard playing baseball. He holds the bat in one hand and the ball in the other, and before throwing up the ball and swinging at it, he announces out loud, "The great hitter is up to bat." He then throws the ball up, swings, and misses. The boy picks up the ball and says, "The greatest hitter in the world is up to bat again." He throws the ball up again, swings, and misses. The boy picks up the ball, shakes his head and states, "The greatest hitter in the history of the game is up to bat." He throws the ball up, swings, and again misses. Now the boy reaches down, grabs the ball and before throwing it up again exclaims, "The world's best batter ever, anywhere, is up and batting against a *very* good pitcher."

Funny, but sometimes life seems to "throw us a bone," and we come across a great idea that seems to be *the* solution for a particular problem we are having. It just "fits."

Maybe you are convinced, by reading this far, that self-talk could change you in such a way as to cause you to become more successful in many areas of your life.

But you might still have this lingering thought: what if this is just a lot of mumbo jumbo, some untested, unscientific psychological trick that sounds good in theory, but doesn't really work in the real world?

I wondered that, too, when I first ran across it, and, being the skeptic that I am, by nature, I wanted to find out if this new idea had any real-world track record.

Here are some of the famous people that I ran across in my research that have used self-talk to change their lives for the better.

Scott Adams and Dilbert

Scott Adams, creator of the hugely successful cartoon strip Dilbert, is a great believer in affirmations. But rather than say them to himself, he likes to write them out. When he was a struggling cartoonist, he began to write out fifteen times every day, "I will be the most successful cartoonist in the world." No matter what happened or how disappointed he was, he made the time to follow through with this practice.

It certainly worked. The struggling cartoonist is now indeed one of the most successful cartoonists in the world. As of 1998, he had an estimated 150 million readers in thirty-nine countries, and the wildly popular Dilbert comic strip now appears in more than 1,500 newspapers.

Roger Clemens, Baseball Star

When it comes to dominance, few pitchers in baseball history compare to New York Yankees' fireballer Roger Clemens.

When he was a young man, his brother would hear him say to himself, over and over again, "One day, I will be an All-Star pitcher and will appear on the cover of Sports Illustrated magazine."

Roger's incredible rise in baseball, as one of the all-time great pitchers, was the featured cover story in Sports Illustrated Magazine on May 12, 1986.

Arnold Talks To Himself!

When he was a teenager, Arnold Schwarzenegger used to tell others (and thus, his brain) that he would become a world famous, award-winning bodybuilder. Some of his close friends at the time say that's all he ever talked about. He would strut around in the gym saying things like "I am a champion body-builder, and I will be the next Mr. Universe." He was so adamant about this that some of his fellow bodybuilders thought he was an egomanic—a braggart and a blow-hard.

But after winning the Mr. Universe contest (five times!) and the Mr. Olympia contest (seven times!) and the Mr. World contest, Arnold Schwarzenegger became what he thought about—and talked to himself about—the most recognized name in bodybuilding in the world.

But he wasn't satisfied with that. He then began telling his friends and acquaintances that his next goal was to become one of Hollywood's top box-office action heroes. Again, they all thought he was just being a bit boastful. But Arnold kept telling others that he would be a star, and, by telling others, of course, he was programming his brain to carry out his goal.

He then applied the same principles to creating a political career, and got elected as the Governor of California. What do you think? Did his self-talk work?

Muhammad Ali, Boxer

Muhammad Ali was one of the greatest boxers of all time. But before he became "The Greatest," before his name became known around the world, he was just another struggling boxer, trying to break into the big time.

As early as sixteen years old Ali was introducing himself with the words, "I'm Cassius Marcellus Clay*; I'm the Golden Gloves Champion of Louisville, Kentucky; someday I'm gonna be heavyweight champion of the world; and I'm gonna be famous." [*Cassius Clay changed his name to Muhammad Ali in 1964 after winning the Heavyweight Championship of the world.]

Before his match with Sonny Liston he said something to the press that startled everyone present: "I am the greatest." Simple, direct, positive and in the present tense. Arrogant? Boastful? Yes, both.

But the fact is, that he actually believed it, whether the rest of the world believed it or not. And although the press scoffed at this bold statement, when he won the fight, they then printed this as the headline in many major newspapers across America.

Later, Ali began to make even bolder statements. As he toured the world as the heavyweight champion, he not only continued to say "I am the greatest," but began predicting in which round he would knock out his opponent. In all but two cases, he was right.

Again, there is power in speaking the thing that you wish to come about.

Wayne Gretsky, Hockey Star

When Wayne Gretsky first started working on his goal to become a star hockey player, he was told that he did not weigh enough, and that he would not survive on the ice rink.

Gretsky ignored the nay-sayers and kept his mind focused on becoming a star player. He would simply affirm, over and over to himself, "I go where the hockey puck's going." This is an example of very specific self-talk that showed he was totally committed to the sport. He wound up creating a multi-million dollar career and did, indeed, become a star on the ice rink.

Dr. Wayne Dyer, Author

Dr. Dyer is the author of a number of best-selling books (probably best known for *Your Erroneous Zones*). Long before he became a best-selling author, he told his colleagues at St. John's University, "I am going to be a best-selling author."

They smiled and nodded. But to date, he has published and sold more than 58 million books.

The list of famous successes goes on and on...

I could give you dozens of illustrations of now-famous people who were considered failures by their peers. Many went bankrupt—several times—and then bounced back to become successful, happy, famous individuals. Erin Brockovich, Sam Donaldson, Bill Walton, Steve Allen, Billy Idol, Pat Boone, Ed Asner, Tony Curtis . . . and many more have shown the world that they could, and did, become what they thought about. Whether or not they ever even heard the term "self-talk," they, in fact, reprogrammed their brain for success and, in many cases, turned their lives around.

For instance, Oprah Winfrey was told by her boss at a local television station that she was "not fit for TV." She programmed in the opposite belief—and she won. Oprah is now one of the most beloved and successful women in television—not to mention, she's a billionaire.

Babe Ruth spent his childhood years in an orphanage, and then struck out 1,330 times as a baseball player—on his way to baseball immortality (714 home runs!).

In 1933, Walter Cronkite was told by a radio station manager that he would never make it as a radio announcer. He became one of the world's most recognizable and trusted voices.

In 1954, Elvis Presley was fired from the Grand Ole Opry after only one performance. He was told by the manager, "You ain't goin' nowhere, son. Better get your job back drivin' a truck."

112

They all had one thing in common.

The stories of famous people who started out in life with nothing, and then failed in many areas of their lives many times before becoming successful, all have one thing in common: you can bet that the self-talk that went on in their mind was not the negative, self-defeating self-talk that most people indulge in constantly.

They all told themselves, over and over again, that they *could* accomplish whatever it was that they set out to accomplish. That they *would* become the person they envisioned in their minds.

Sir Edmund Hillary wanted to climb Mount Everest and, after three failed attempts, finally succeeded. Do you think he was telling himself, "I'm such an idiot. It's obvious I can't possibly make it to the top of Mount Everest. Why, that's impossible for any human to accomplish. No one else has ever done it. Why do I think I can do it? I should just move on with my life and forget it."

I'm sure, if we could have listened in to his self-talk before his fourth climb, we would have heard a very different dialogue—one that sounded something like this:

"I may have failed to reach the top three times, but I have learned from my mistakes. Now, I know *exactly* what I need to do to get to the peak this time. Why, with the right weather conditions, *anyone* with my skills could make it to the top of this mountain. I am strong, healthy, and I now know exactly how to make it all the way! And I will prove to everyone that it *is* possible to climb to the top. I can do it. I know I can. And *noth-*

ing will stop me this time!"

Even after all these stories of proven success, you may still be saying something to yourself like, "Yeah, right, Patrick. It worked for them, but they're all special. They had something I don't have—I'll never be a star!"

It's true that all these examples had fame in common as well as positive self-talk. But there are countless examples of people out there just like you, with everyday, "ordinary" lives, who have had success in every area of their lives with this method.

In the next chapter, you'll hear directly from a few of them, in their own words, about what self-talk has done in their lives.

Relentless, repetitive self talk is what changes our self-image.

—Denis Waitley

12

What Has This Done for "Real People"?

The power of self-talk should not be discounted in stories like these about real people, whether famous or as yet unknown. Remember, by telling others what you intend to accomplish, you are also programming your brain to carry out your goals and desires. I'm a believer in this process because it changed my life completely—and if you want to change, too, you can.

One of the most significant areas of success with self-talk in people's lives is in the area of health and fitness. It goes without saying that if you have a challenge with your health, you should always continue to work with your physician and treatment plan—but it might well benefit you to add the power of positive self-talk to your arsenal.

To show you how powerful this can be, let me share with you some of the research that has been done in the field of mind-body connection for health.

Many of our real, physical illnesses come from our thought processes.

In one of our training classes for my company, our guest was a neurosurgeon. She quoted a statistic that surprised us. She said that as much as 75% of all illnesses are self-induced!

That doesn't mean those illnesses are not real. It doesn't mean you don't really have a rash, or an ulcer, or whatever. It means that in many cases, the stress in our lives causes our bodies to manifest many physical illnesses that we would not otherwise have.

And, we are told by psychologists that as much as 77% of everything we think is negative, counterproductive, and works against us.

Now I don't know if that's true or not. Let's say it's only 25%. That's still a lot of negative inputs that you have to overcome in life, if that's true. It's no wonder so many of us are sick—or think we are. Hypochondriacs are not hypochondriacs because they want to be; it's because their brains somehow make sure that they are literally, physically sick.

For instance, a close friend of mine was under such stress at one time that he could just look at his arm and a welt would appear. His mind caused his body to reflect the stress in his life, with a physical symptom that was very real.

In a study in Japan, they took a group of people and rubbed leaves on their arms, telling them that it was poison ivy. Half of them were rubbed with some innocuous leaf that wouldn't do anything to anyone under normal circumstances. But, guess how many of them broke out with poison ivy symptoms? That's right—all of them.

The point is, our minds are more powerful than we think they are. So powerful, in fact, that what you believe most can literally make the difference between life and death.

It's true if you think it is . . .

A few years ago, a man was traveling across the country by sneaking rides on freight trains. One particular night, he climbed into what looked like a boxcar and closed the door. Somehow, the door locked shut and he was trapped inside. When his eyes adapted to the dark, he realized that he was inside a refrigerated boxcar. He began to shiver, and his teeth soon began to chatter. All the noise he made inside the car failed to attract anyone's attention. He hopelessly gave up and lay down on the floor of the railroad car.

As he tried to fight against the cold, he was overcome by hypothermia and fell asleep—never to wake again. Sometime the next day, repairmen from the railroad opened the door of the refrigerated boxcar and found the man dead. He looked like someone who had frozen to death.

But the problem was this: *the refrigeration units on the boxcar had not worked for some time.* The repairmen had come to repair those units. The temperature had not gone down below fifty degrees during the night. The man died because he believed that he was freezing to death! His mind was so convinced that he was going to freeze to death, that his body carried out the instructions.

The good news is that the same "mind power" that can cause illness, can also help to ease or even cure it.

Remission From Terminal Cancer

In his book, *Getting Well Again*, Dr. Carl Simonton and his wife Stephanie document the results of their research into the way the mind works to heal the body. Not only have people experienced complete remission from terminal cancer, but some have also used the same process to experience complete remission of arthritis, asthmas, and other painful diseases.

People who were expected to live less than a year have not only outlived the prognosis by at least twice that; they have also lived a more active, normal life. The process that Dr. Simonton used was a variation of the self-talk we have been discussing. Along with any medical treatment, this physician asked his patients to spend time daily talking to their bodies, telling them that the white blood cells in their body were attacking and defeating the evil cancer cells. The results reported were miraculous.

Even as you read this, similar research is being conducted in major hospitals around the globe, because of the dramatic and promising results.

Hyperactive Children Calm Down

One of the most interesting applications of self-talk is in work with hyperactive, impulsive children. Dr. Donald Meichenbaum is one of the founders of the "cognitive revolution" in psychotherapy. In his work, he would first model for the child the task that needed to be done. While performing the task, the doctor or the adult would talk out loud to himself, telling himself what to do.

Then the child was asked to attempt to perform the same task while instructing himself out loud, just as the adult had done. In the research, a very interesting thing happened over time. The verbal instructions the child gave to himself were first mumbled, then whispered and then internalized into private speech or thoughts, with the child simply mouthing the words.

A variety of tasks were used, from the simple task of drawing a line, to the complex task of learning to drive a car. In every case, the child became less hyperactive and impulsive, simply by utilizing the positive effects of self-talk and self-direction.

How Self-Talk Helps With Depression

More remarkable results came from an experiment by Dr. Aaron Beck, one of the early theorists who advocated the treatment of depression by changing a person's self-talk.

Dr. Beck recruited a number of people experiencing similar levels of depression and divided them into two groups. One group was treated for 12 weeks with an antidepressant medication; the other group was treated for 12 weeks with therapy focused only on their inner self-talk. This second group received no medication.

At the end of the 12 weeks, the results were quite unexpected, especially in showing the significant amount of differences between the two groups. In the group receiving only the medication, approximately 20 per cent showed complete recovery, and almost 33 per cent of the group dropped out before completing the 12 weeks.

In the group working only on their inner self-talk, over *75 per cent* showed complete recovery, and only 10 per cent of the group either dropped out or failed to show any improvement!

In a follow-up of the participants a year later, by the way, the gains recorded at the end of the 12 weeks were maintained by both groups. Medication helped some people, but positive self-talk helped even more! Attitude is everything, or at least, in the case of depression, almost everything.

Hundreds of Patients Cured, With a Simple Phrase

Emile Coue, the 19th century French professor, became a pioneer of positive affirmation techniques, curing hundreds of patients in Europe and North America by teaching his patients to repeat the following simple affirmation, each morning and evening: "Every day, in every way, I'm getting better and better." Using this simple affirmation alone, the healing results of Dr. Coue were nothing less than spectacular.

How do you explain it? The body responds to what the mind is hearing. It is automatic, and there is nothing as powerful as the mind/body connection.

Real Success in the Lives of Real People

Just in case you're still not convinced of the power of this method, let me share with you some direct quotes from the lives of real people who were happy to let me tell their self-talk success stories when they learned I was writing this book. The hardest part of the process was to choose which ones to include, since there were so many! (These are quotes from actual letters received in recent months by Dr. Helmstetter and myself, and are used by permission.)

Here is just a sample of the kind of results you can expect when you begin to put self-talk reprogramming to work in your life:

Bret from Chicago overcame shyness:

"I went from being depressed (at one point I was on both Prozac and Paxil), frustrated and so shy I was unable to ask a stranger for the time (much to my wife's dismay) to being able to talk to crowds and meet new people on a regular basis. This process took a couple of years but accelerated when I went from speaking my self-talk to listening to self-talk on CD…thank you for the work you've done!"

Jonathan is much more fun to be around:

"My story is quite remarkable. I have a long history of severe illness. But, since using your 2 CDs "Personal and Professional Success," my life has changed dramatically. I am involved in multi-level marketing and as a lone inventor am now focusing on my third project. Those around me have all noticed a great change in my level of positivism and I'm much more fun to be with now. Things are working out so well for me that I'm going to appear on TV soon reading my own poetry. I thank you most sincerely."

Phyllis has improved her health:

"I'm using your self-talk programs to help with my recent diagnosis of MS. When I was still in the hospital (only 2 weeks ago), I was encouraged to do as much as I could on my own— and I did! The nurses would cheer me on, even saying "nothing can keep her down!" My doctors and nurses have been amazed at my positive attitude and believe it has been one of the keys to my rapid recovery from an acute attack, and is one of the elements that makes my prognosis for the future so great (as long as I can learn to manage stress better and follow my treatment plan, I can expect to continue working for "another 30 years" and live a relatively normal life.) Unless I tell someone, they would not even know I have MS! THANK YOU for bringing the gift of self-talk to me!"

Rick from Maui recovered from depression:

"I had originally read your book about 3 years ago. At that time, I was so depressed I didn't want to wake up the next day. I would read the self-talk in that book over and over every single day. I remember times at work when I was so down and felt like there was no end in sight, I would go into the restroom and pull out my book. I would read it over and over until I felt like I could continue. I am very fortunate to have found this book. It has taken me from being fully depressed to being empowered. Self-talk has done for me what no medicine could ever do. I now live in Hawaii and run a successful business. I listen to the self-talk CDs every single day. Self-talk has truly changed my life!"

Srinivas, a software engineer found a new job:

"The self-talk (power of the spoken word) concept has helped me in my life in many ways, in all aspects of my life. Three years ago I faced a situation where many people were losing their jobs. It happened to me, too. I had just read your book, and applied its principles to get my next job. I practiced the self-talk for four weeks regularly, day in and day out.

Every time I had a situation, I just set a goal and spoke as though the results I wanted were already happening. You won't believe it! Even though the market was turned upside down and everyone was complaining, I got four jobs at the same time! If we were not introduced to this concept, I don't know where my family and I would be today. And that's only the beginning. I can write hundreds of examples of how self-talk has changed our lives."

Daniel overcomes physical challenges:

"Many would consider the condition I was born with a disability. I have limited use of my arms and legs that results in a great challenge to dress, feed, and bathe myself. I can personally testify to the powerful techniques Mr. Phillips shares in this life-changing book. Because I have put these principles to work in my own life, I am currently the CEO of my own retail cosmetics/skincare company and I am also a professional motivational speaker. This book is a must if you want to learn how to embrace success and overcome challenges in your life."

What about you?

All this is well and good, but the only thing that really matters is if *you* put this secret into effect in your own life.

If all these people were helped by merely changing their self-talk, just think what you could do with your life if you could somehow grab hold of your brain and change the way you think about success, money and health.

If you have been filling your mind with negative programs all your life, then you might need to reexamine how you have been talking to yourself. Maybe, just maybe, you've been sabotaging yourself without even knowing it.

If you keep on saying
things are going to be bad,
you have a good chance
of being a prophet.

—**Isaac Singer**

13

How We Sabotage Ourselves

Sometimes our brains have been programmed so thoroughly by our old inner self-talk that it rebels against any new programming that comes along. Let me show you what I'm talking about.

Let's say you have decided to reprogram your brain to stop smoking. As part of your new input, you say to yourself something like the following: "I am a non-smoker. I like taking care of my body and putting only good, healthy things into it."

Your brain, hearing this for the first time, is quite taken back by this new input. It is used to hearing things like, "Man, this cigarette tastes good. It seems to calm my nerves and cut my hunger. I like the way it makes me feel. It relaxes me and helps me de-stress."

The brain's immediate response to the new, good input, "I am a non-smoker" might be something along these lines: "I am too a smoker! And even if I did stop, I'd probably gain 50 pounds overnight. Besides, it's one of the few pleasures I have in life. It's too hard to stop."

But remember, your old negative self-talk is usually a mixture of half-truths, poor logic, and distortions of reality that perpetuates negative emotions such as pessimism, guilt, fear, and anxiety.

It often occurs in times of emotional turmoil, or when we are going through stress or a personal transition—the very kind of situation where you're used to reaching for a cigarette.

So, what can you do about this negative response to your new inner self-talk? Simple.

Ignore Your Negative Programs

That's right. Ignore them. No need to worry about this negative response. This inner dialogue, as you will learn, is quite normal, especially if you've gotten in the habit of telling yourself negative things whenever you hear someone say something positive.

If you just ignore this initial negative response to your new programming, you will find that your brain, through the magic of repetition, will begin to adjust itself to this new positive input.

When you catch yourself repeating the old negative programs, take a deep breath, relax, and remove yourself from the situation. Get up and stretch, or take a walk, or get a drink of water, in order to interrupt your train of thought and get out of the negative rut.

Begin to replace your negative thoughts with realistic, positive thoughts. Soon you'll stop the negativity in mid-sentence

. . . and begin to replace it with positive new self-talk programming that can change your life.

For the example of trying to stop smoking, if you keep working on changing your programs, you will begin to hear something like this: "These things really don't taste that good. I would probably stop this nagging cough and breathe easier at night if I could become a non-smoker."

This type of response might not happen until your brain has had the "good input" several dozen times—or even a hundred times or more. But with the simplified method of getting the new programming into your brain (through the magic of CD listening), if you just continue to put the good stuff in, your brain will eventually accept the new input as *fact*.

Then, after a hundred more new inputs, your brain might react with this inner dialogue: "This is really a nasty habit. I suppose I could see myself as a non-smoker...someday."

A month later: "These things are bitter and they stain my teeth yellow and make my breath stink. I don't need these to calm my nerves. I am taking charge of my life in other areas; I can at least skip this one cigarette."

After another month of reprogramming, your mind might be responding like this to the new input: "I am a non-smoker in training! I do feel better after cutting down to one pack a day. I'm going to cut down to a half-pack starting today. I'm breathing better and sleeping better because I don't cough as much. I really am becoming a non-smoker!"

I thought money was evil.

As I grew up I heard these negative things about money: *"You have to work hard to make money," "Money doesn't grow on trees," "Money is the root of all evil," "We live on a fixed income," "We can not afford to have nicer things," "We live hand to mouth," "Life is hard and then you die; you better have a good insurance policy so your family can afford to bury you,"."Don't be greedy," "We have to work hard and live in poverty because God loves us."*

Sound familiar to you? Most likely, you have a few scripts of your own to add to my list. It's no wonder that I (and possibly you) grew up to become poverty-minded. We had no choice in the matter.

Remember, the brain has no choice in the matter.

The good news is that once you begin the good programming your brain will eventually accept the new input, over time, without failure. Your only job is to play the CDs daily (or say the words, out loud, several times a day).

Your brain will actually form new neural pathways as you give it the new programming, the new inner self-talk. It is like recording a new message over an old magnetic tape. The new message simply replaces the old. In the case of your brain, it just takes enough times for the new messages to be re-recorded over the old messages.

But it will happen.

The reason I'm telling you about this negative feedback is that, once you realize this is a normal response, it will not discourage you or dishearten you in any way. When it happens to you, simply smile, knowing that your brain is totally under your control, and it cannot prevail over the repetitive onslaught of positive input you will be giving it over the next few weeks.

In the next chapter, I'm going to help you think of this whole process in a very simple way that will make it very clear to you. It has to do with that little genie that is always bottled up inside of you. We're going to let him out of the bottle . . .

You, alone, are painting your own canvas,
thought by thought, choice by choice.

—Oprah Winfrey

14

Your Own Personal Genie

Imagine what your life could be like if you had your own personal Genie inside you, just waiting for instructions and ready to grant your every wish.

Of course, if it were this easy we would all live in mansions and zip around in Mercedes. But we can give our Genie mental programming instructions and he will carry them out to the letter.

If you're not where you want to be in life, what commands are you giving your Genie?

Your Three Wishes

Want to change your life? Here's the quick answer: pay closer attention to your thoughts and the instructions you give your Genie. If that sounds too simple, just grab your magic lamp and read on.

Sometimes we think what we say to ourselves doesn't matter, that these are just random or fleeting thoughts. The fact is, what you say to yourself (your Genie) really does matter and it will determine your fate for the day, this week . . . your entire life.

Where can you find this Genie? He is your subconscious mind. And here's the rub: we don't have a choice as to whether or not we give him instructions. He pays attention to our every thought. Our only point of control is the type of instructions we provide.

If you're thinking, "Life sucks. This is really lousy," your Genie hears that. You may not think he is affected by this negative self-talk, but Genie takes it all in and attempts to give you what you have requested. He is very disciplined that way.

The trouble is, he's not good at deciphering moods, doubts, and fears. In fact, your Genie has no reasoning capabilities whatsoever. That is your domain. His only job is to obey your commands.

When you tell yourself, "Today is going to be a bad day because that's the way my 'luck' runs," your Genie hears that and says, "Okay, I have received your wish. Here is your bad day!"

Of course, you didn't mean for him to take that literally, and you may not have even realized you used up a wish when you had that thought.

Think about the last time you balled up a wad of paper and threw it across the room into the trash can. Bull's eye! It felt so good to make a shot of that distance with deadly accuracy that you decided to do it again.

This time you give it some thought. That little nagging

part of your brain you thought was asleep starts telling you, "That first shot was luck. You can't do that again." And sure enough, your next shot bounces off the rim onto the floor.

You immediately spring up and grab the wad of paper, not dropping it in the trash, but taking it back to the spot from where you missed to try again. It's the Trash Can Game, and we've all played it. It's also an excellent example of the Genie inside us, executing the commands we provide him.

Be careful what you tell yourself—your Genie is listening.

We must be very careful what we tell ourselves, because our Genie, as wonderful as he is, cannot distinguish our real intent. Everything we say passes to him without going through any filters.

For example, you may tell yourself, "This is stupid. I'm not going to try very hard to do my best because I'll probably fail anyway."

Your intent may have been to give yourself a cushion to fall back on just in case you didn't do as well as you hoped—but the trouble with giving yourself that 'out' is that your Genie will do everything in his power to grant your request of failure. He is undermining your ultimate desire to be the best you can be. He doesn't mean to do this, of course; he is just following the orders you gave him.

Everything you see in the space you are now in was once a thought in someone's mind. The chair you are sitting in, the car you drive, the television you watch—none of these would exist had they not originated in the mind of their creator. The thing to recognize is that we are all creators. We are the creators of our own destiny, the authors of our own story.

The story I created for my life, up until I was 45 years old, was that I wasn't very smart. Neither of my parents was well educated, and I hated school, wanting to finish my education by the age of 16. In fact, I dropped out of high school and then finished through correspondence.

The three decades that followed found me comfortable with that story, if not somewhat unfulfilled. It took me thirty years to realize I had the power to change my life; to write a new chapter to alter the direction of the story altogether.

Once I recognized this, I wrote chapters into my life I didn't even think were possible. I went on to start a financial services company that did over ten million dollars a year in sales for several years straight. I became more successful in every area of my life than I ever thought I could be—and all because I decided to clearly instruct my Genie to create success for me instead of failure.

We all have this "magical" power.

Sometimes we don't even know that our minds have the power to make us successful, much less take responsibility for that power or that process. We tend to pay more attention to the events in our lives. When we react to something that has happened to us, we label it and then attach a story to it.

Good, bad, exhilarating, depressing, rewarding or unfair, we make a note of it. We give these stories to our Genie for safekeeping. He stores them and will dutifully recover these accounts of events just as we have filed them.

When we come upon a similar event in our life, sometimes years after Genie first filed the original input, he quickly shows us what to do next, based on what has happened in our past.

At first glance, this sounds well and good. You have a living encyclopedia at your disposal along with your own "Genie librarian" to tell you the correct response in any given situation. The problem with this automatic, programmed response based on our programming is that, in many cases, those responses are no longer valid.

We may have matured and outgrown a conditioned response, yet we continue to act out inappropriate behavior—no matter how self-destructive—because we have programmed ourselves to do so.

You are a result of the sum total of your programs.

Your life today is the culmination of every thought you've ever had. Once you embrace this concept, once you recognize you have created your world and take responsibility for it, you should also realize you have the power to change your world by simply changing your thoughts. You can rewrite your story through new experiences and different responses to your new and improved life.

Best selling author, Neale Donald Walsch, talks about our three levels of thought and creation:

That which you think of, but thereafter never speak of,
creates at one level.

That which you think and speak of creates at another level.

That which you think, speak, and do becomes
made manifest in your reality.

Walsch goes on to say that if our lives are going to 'take off', we must become very clear about what we want to be, do and have. Get rid of all negative thoughts. Forget all fears and doubts.

When we are very clear about what we want, we must think about it often and think about nothing else. We need to take ownership, and begin speaking our thoughts as truths in order to create the desired result in our lives.

Personal Coach Christen Murphy says, "What we focus on, grows. We become what we think about most, so choose your thoughts well."

She also states, "As humans, we like to make sense of our surroundings. Positive or negative, either way, we get to be 'right' about our life."

The question is, what do *you* want to be right about? Positive and negative emotions cannot occupy the mind at the same time. Remember, your personal Genie will always respond to your thoughts and unspoken requests with, "Your wish is my command."

Feed your mental Genie positive, supportive and well-nourished thoughts, and you will live a live of prosperity, abundance, and untold riches.

And if you do this, you won't need to make your third and final wish a request for three more wishes!

Thought is action in rehearsal.

—**Sigmund Freud**

15

Ten Important Things to Remember

When you consider that you spend infinitely more time with your "self"—listening to your internal dialogue—than you do listening to any other person in your life, it pays to keep these important points in mind:

1. Your self-talk is constant.

What you say to yourself in your head goes on 24/7. When you think about it, this is tremendously more input into your life than any other person could possibly contribute. Isn't it important that you learn how to keep that self-talk positive and upbeat, at least most of the time?

2. Your self-talk takes place in real time.

Your self-talk is a running commentary that never stops. If it's good self-talk that's going on in your head, that's the best 'friend' you can have.

But if you've gotten the wrong programs along the way and haven't done anything about it yet, you're stuck instead with negative, self-defeating statements going on all day long inside your head: "I could never learn to sell," "I'm a fat pig," "Women can't stand me," "All men are animals," "I'm a clumsy klutz," "I'll never make big money," etc.

These thoughts are happening in your head in real time, as the situation is unfolding around you. And the situation you create is entirely up to you and what you choose to program into your mind from now on.

3. Your body reacts as if your self-talk is real.

What you say to yourself in your head has physiological outcomes. For example, when you think, "This report is horrible, and they're going to laugh me out of the classroom, and I'm probably going to fail because of this, and then my parents will kick me out of the house," your body will respond to the negative program. Your palms sweat, your heart beats faster, and a surge of adrenalin pours into your system. The end result of having the wrong programming is that you don't function as well, and put your body under tremendous stress.

This makes it difficult for you at the moment, and then creates habitual thought patterns that replay in the future, creating a cumulative level of stress that can lead to illness. All the research points to the same conclusion: you *literally* become what you think about, and your health is no exception.

4. Your self-talk programs are heavily influenced by what you attribute things to.

According to Dr. Phil McGraw, better known to most of us as simply "Dr. Phil," our programs are influenced by our sense of "locus-of-control"—what we attribute things to. There are basically three choices: everything's my fault; everything's someone else's fault; or it happened because of chance or luck.

The important point here is that if you want to create lasting change, you need to once and for all take personal responsibility for your mental programs and your resulting actions in order to become the success you want to be.

5. Your self-talk is tremendously overpowering.

Your old programs of negative self-talk are so powerful that they can overwhelm any other input, including reality itself.

For instance, if your old self-talk tells you that women don't like to date you, your head will be so full of that at the party that you'll probably fail to even notice the rather shy but extremely appealing young woman who does her best to get your attention and initiate a conversation.

If you don't change your programs, you'll continue to be stuck with the same old results—regardless of the positive reality of the situation.

6. Negative self-talk gets the loudest when you need it the least.

When the pressure's on, we revert to default mode. For instance, everyone has one side of the brain that is dominant. Each of us is able to use both hemispheres, but when learning something new, which is stressful, we all default to the dominant hemisphere.

By the same token, when feeling stressed we hype up the negative self-talk, which is—to say the least—self-defeating. We're bringing in the negative self-talk because we think we can't do something, then it tells us we can't do something, and then we make sure we can't!

In order for your positive new programs to get louder than the old negatives, you've got to stay with it long enough for the new information to take hold. We've all heard that it takes 21 days to change a habit—and that's because that's how long it takes for the new programs to begin making changes in your brain. So make sure that when it's time to change your programs, you make the commitment to stick with the process to give it time to work.

7. Self-talk can be a major life force.

Your internal self-talk is relentless and ever-present. That's one reason some psychologists say, "Be adamantly and relentlessly self-forgiving."

Most of us do not reach adulthood with self-talk that says, "I'm very good at selling and sell best under pressure," or

"Most women like me and I have always dated lovely women though some of the relationships didn't work out." In at least one area, most of us have some really negative self-talk tapes running, that continue to strongly affect our lives in everything we do.

If you want different results, you have to get different programs—and they will affect your life just as strongly, but this time, in the positive.

8. You talk to yourself in ways you would never think of talking to someone else.

If you walked up to someone else and said, "You're a stupid, worthless S.O.B.", they would recoil in horror and pain or lash back at you with verbal or physical abuse.

However, it's not uncommon to have that kind of self-talk going on inside yourself about you. You know in your heart that if you talked to someone else this way, it would exacerbate a bad situation, and not solve anything, as well as being unkind and possibly untrue; and yet we sometimes talk that way to ourselves.

You can make the choice to always treat yourself at least as well as you treat other people—and that transition starts by getting rid of the old programs that have been in your way. If you want to feel better about yourself, start with the right new self-talk, and see what happens next.

9. Ultimately, if you have negative self-talk, you create a toxic internal environment.

Considering that self-talk goes on 24/7, and also that many people aren't consciously aware of it—or aware it can be changed—as the months and years go by, you create a sort of closed-loop toxic waste area in your mind and body. In the worst-case scenario, every time you dip into this area of your mind you pull up something negative, and defeat yourself, and then throw that back into the cesspool.

It's particularly important for your ongoing health and well-being that you correct this process before it leads to serious illness. But now that you know about it, you can choose to program in the right new self-talk of a healthy mind, body and life—and that's exactly what you'll get.

10. You need to listen to your body, because it definitely listens to you!

Such a toxic inner environment created by bad programming is what causes headaches, pain, depression, anxiety, poor functioning, and a self-defeating spiral into failure. Any degree of negativity from yourself to yourself is more than you need. If you make the choice to change, and follow through on your decision, you will set yourself free from the toxic effects of negativity once and for all.

How to get started TODAY

In the Appendix you will find a number of scripts of self-talk phrases that will give you a strong "beginner" reference book of self-talk. Any of these will help you specifically reprogram some of the most important areas that affect your success.

Remember, repetition is the key to your success with reprogramming. The more often you read your new self-talk, see it, or hear it, the better it will work, and the faster your programs will change.

To be sure you get the most repetition in the easiest way possible, I recommend that you do what I did and listen to the self-talk.

You can purchase a portable cassette recorder and record these scripts yourself, or ask a trusted friend or loved-one to do so for you. Listen to them as you go to sleep, when you are getting ready for work, or while driving. Listen as often as you can. Remember, it takes a lot of repetition of the good programming to block out the old, bad programming.

All of the scripts are also available on Professional Self-Talk CDs—the same exact kind of self-talk I listened to, and turned my life around. (The scripts in the following section are from the Lifetime Library of Positive Self-Talk, Self-Talk for Weight Loss, and Personal and Professional Success. All material is copyrighted by Dr. Shad Helmstetter and used by permission.)

You can order these and other self-talk programs (including special self-talk for your kids and teens) from:

www.howtoreprogram.com

I sincerely wish you well as you continue your journey to becoming a better "you." And I hope this book helps you along the way. Use it as a tool to strengthen you as you pursue your most important goals, and to help you get past the old programs of doubt long enough to see the potential you were born with in the first place.

I, and many others, have changed our lives by changing the way we talk to ourselves. So can you—starting today.

Appendix

Self-Talk for Personal and Professional Success

This is self-talk for making the choice to achieve.
My success is up to me. I know it, and I create it.

I know that success is a choice, and I choose to achieve.

I choose to live up to my best.

I know that my achievement is up to me.
I take charge of my success.

I know that my success is not up to my past. My success is up
to me, now. I am in control of my present, and I am creating
my future. My success is up to me.

Right now, this moment, for this day and for every day here-
after, I give myself permission to succeed.

I create positive opportunities in everything I do.

I enjoy making my life work.

Making my life work, in the best possible way, is something I do every day.

I know the three most positive things that I want most. Right now, I see them in my mind, and I choose to create them in my life.

I visualize my success every day. I see myself achieving my goals, and I am creating my success right now.

I turn my goals into action. I know what needs to be done, and I do it. I take action.

I choose to be strong. I am always stronger than any obstacle that stands in my way.

I always expect, and anticipate, the most positive outcome of anything that I do.

I have strong self-respect, great self-control, and positive, winning self-esteem.

I choose to live my life right, and every day of my life counts. This moment, right now, is important to me.

I take the time to succeed. I do what it takes to achieve.

Right now, I choose to do next, the one thing that will help me the most.

SELF-TALK FOR SELF-ESTEEM

I like myself. I choose to like who I am.

I feel good about myself. I like the way I think. I like the things I do. I like the way I live my life.

I have self-confidence. I know myself, and I am proud of the person I have chosen to be.

An accurate description of me would include the words, wonderful, unique, well-liked, positive, self-directed, happy and incredible.

Because I choose to like myself, other people like me too. I care about myself, and I care about them, too.

I am a quality person. I am worthwhile. I deserve to live at my best, and to receive the best from the life I live.

I am attractive. And because I am attractive, I attract the best in everything around me.

People really enjoy my company. They like the way I think. They like the way I express myself— and they like the person I am.

I really deserve good things in my life.

Each morning, I wake up feeling good about myself.

I am happy with the way I see myself each day.
I am proud of the job I am doing, making my life count.

I have a lot to feel good about. I recognize the potential that is within me, and I have made the choice to live it out.

When I look at myself in the mirror, I see someone who has high self-esteem.

How I feel about myself is very important to me, so I make sure that I always find, recognize and acknowledge my best.

I know that I write the script in the creation of my own self. I alone am in charge of who I am.

It is true that I am a unique, special and quality individual. I was born that way, and it's the natural way for me to be.

I am a person who does many things right. I have truth, understanding, creativity, talents and skills within me—and

I see evidence of each of them in the way I live my life each day.

When people look at me, they see a person with good, healthy, positive, strong self-esteem. That's because that's the way I am.

I really like myself. I like myself every minute of every day. I like myself right now, and I am proud of who I am.

SELF-TALK FOR FINANCIAL SUCCESS

I believe that having money and financial strength is good, positive and healthy.

I know that working for, receiving and holding the riches of life is the natural, automatic result of putting forth positive effort.

I believe that attitudes about money and financial strength are always up to the individual, and I alone choose the importance that I place upon money and its value in my life.

I recognize that my financial strength and security, and how much of it I have, is always the result of the choices I make.

I believe that having financial security is completely up to me, and the picture of myself that I create in my own mind.

I choose to remove the limits and the barriers that could have stood in my way, and I create the success that I deserve.

I know that lasting financial success never happens by accident. It is always the result of the right plan, the right actions, and my own determination to succeed.

To me, creating financial success is fun and exciting. It is a pursuit of positive benefits and the greatest rewards.

I recognize that wealth means more to me than the possession of money or material goods. Wealth, to me, means expressing my true potential each day, in every area of my life.

I know that the more aware I am of my ability to succeed, the more success I create.

I believe that there is no mystery to the creation and accumulation of financial strength. I already know I have what it takes to reach my goals, and I work at improving my skills and performance every day.

I recognize that the right to have financial security is not given to some, and withheld from others. Money, security and financial strength are the natural possessions of those who choose to have them.

I believe in the positive values of honesty, integrity, charity and service toward others. Living my life by these values always increases my success and the quality of my life.

I recognize that it is not money itself that creates the benefits in my life. It is the positive utility of my resources that improves both my life, and the lives of those around me.

I believe in sharing my wealth, sharing my joy, sharing myself, and sharing my life.

SELF-TALK FOR POSITIVE RELATIONSHIPS

Positive relationships are an important part of my life. I know that when I care about myself, I am able to care about others, and I care about myself.

I believe in myself, so I can believe in others, too.

Good relationships are a constant source of happiness and enjoyment in my life. I find that my relationships with others make life even richer and more rewarding.

I believe that everyone deserves to have good relationships. I deserve many good things in my life, and I deserve the love, the friendship and the joy that my relationships bring me.

Relationships add immeasurably to the expression of my own self. The person I am is always greater because of the friendships I create.

I know that when you truly care about others, you are never alone. Because I care, I always have friendship, companionship and love in my life.

I recognize that building and keeping a good relationship takes time, and I am always willing to give the time that it takes. I invest in my relationships, and I enjoy the rewards they create in my life.

I understand that creating relationships means taking a risk, but I also know that positive risks create positive results.

Relationships are fun, and I have fun in my life.

Being around others who are full of life and energy creates more life and energy in me.

I get along well with others, because I get along well with myself. I have good relationships with them, because I have a good relationship with me.

I believe in being able to give of myself, but I never do, say, think or give anything that could harm me in any way.

I know how to say yes, and I know how to say no.

I recognize and respect the needs of others, but I also recognize, respect and protect my own needs.

I believe that my relationships create a constant source of healthy, positive anticipation in my day. My relationships with others add immeasurably to my life.

Each time I hear these words and think about their meaning and importance in my life, I recognize the value of other people and my relationships with them.

I create good relationships in my life, and I get better at it every day.

SELF-TALK FOR PERSONAL ORGANIZATION

Being organized, to me, means being in balance and in control of my time and my life.

I believe that having good organizational skills makes life work better. Being organized is an important part of being in control.

I recognize the value of having an organized mind. Thinking sharp, being alert, being in tune and being in touch are important to me.

I recognize controlling my time adds more time to my day, and I like having more time to accomplish the many things I want to do.

I choose to make choices instead of leaving things up to chance. I believe that my time and my space in life are up to me.

I recognize that having balance is an important ingredient in a happy life, and I always pay just the right amount of attention to creating organization and control in my life.

I believe that a life of harmony and balance is the result of a calm, self-directed and uncluttered mind — and that is the way I choose to be.

I know that organization begins with a state of mind. The organization of my time and my life always begins with the management of my own thoughts.

I know that organization is more than having a clean desk and always being on time. To me, being organized is having a sense of order in every part of my life.

Being organized is being in touch with what makes things work best for me.

Organization is the skill that adds to my security and sense of well-being. Organization creates peace of mind in my life.

I understand that instead of organization destroying creativity, organization enhances creativity and gives it the time and the place to grow.

Being organized is recognizing and using the mind at its best. Personal organization is the keystone of personal growth.

The ability to set attainable goals begins with the ability to prioritize and organize.

I know that being in control of my mind and what I do with my mind is one of the most enjoyable and rewarding choices I could ever make.

I recognize that the positive habit of personal organization is the foundation of a successful life.

Taking responsibility for organizing my life is the first step to my success.

SELF-TALK FOR WEIGHT LOSS

I look great, and I feel great. Looking and feeling good is one of the many rewards I receive for keeping myself fit and trim, and I keep myself that way.

I take responsibility for myself. I alone determine how I look, how much I weigh, and how I feel.

I choose to have high self-esteem. I have high self-esteem.

I have fun losing weight and keeping trim, and I'm really proud of the great job I'm doing.

My confidence in who I am, how I look, and how I feel is reflected in everything I do.

Because I am aware of the importance of my own health and fitness, I now spend my time doing those things that help me get more fit, in shape, and reaching my weight loss goals. I begin each day by concentrating and focusing on becoming my new self. I set my goals, I review them each day, I see myself achieving each of them, and I reach them.

I am in control of every action I take, and every movement I make.

I am good at telling myself "no" to anything I should not eat, and immediately replacing the desire to eat with a far

162

greater desire to reach my goal, to live my dream, to like myself, to stay on target, and make today count!

I never let anyone, at any time, influence me or convince me to forget my goal, for even a moment.

From the moment I awake in the morning, to the moment I go to sleep at night, I am in control of what I do.

The achievement of reaching my best weight, my best health, my best shape, and my greatest fitness, is an achievement that is worth every moment that I put into it.

All of my habits create good health.

I reward myself in ways that are healthy, and build even more self-respect and self-esteem. I think, act, feel and live differently now. Right now, and at all times, I see myself in a whole new, trim, attractive way.

When I sit down to eat at any meal, I say to myself, "I live best when I eat less!"

Maintaining my weight is easy for me now. I have learned to eat right, exercise more, and keep my mind and my body fit and healthy.

SELF-TALK FOR QUALITY OF LIFE

I am a person who believes in the quality of life. That's because I am a quality person.

I enjoy my life. I'm glad to be here, and I'm having fun being who I am.

For me, even the smallest moments and the littlest things in my life count.

I have peace of mind, and I make sure that I always see the best in every situation. I keep things in perspective. I keep my optimism up, and I refuse to let things get me down.

I am practical and realistic, but I am always able to believe in the best. I have faith, and I put my faith to work in every part of my life.

I believe in my life, and I believe in who I am.
I like myself right now. I'm working at getting better every day, but I like who I am right now, today.

I like being happy. I am good at creating joy in my life.

I see life as a remarkable adventure. I look forward to greeting each new day, and looking forward to what it will bring.

I am always open to new things. I am awake, I am aware, I

am inquisitive, and I am alive!

I am my own person. I live my life by my own direction and design, and never by the negative or limited opinions of others.

I set my own limits. I choose where I want to go. I set my own course. I get myself moving, and I enjoy the journey.

I know how to dream. I visualize and create a life of incredible quality, peace of mind, and fulfillment. And what I create in my mind, I create in my life.

A description of me would include the words, happy, active, alive, enthusiastic, curious, optimistic, eager, fulfilled, and living a quality life.

I am never afraid to try. And because I believe in myself and enjoy the adventure that each day brings, I am never afraid to fail—and I am never afraid to succeed.

I am truly alive. Instead of waiting to live my life for some other day, I live my life every moment of every day, and I make every moment count.

Resources

BOOKS

Ball, Carolyn M. *Claiming Your Self-Esteem*. Berkeley:
Celestial Arts Publishing, 1990.

Bassett, Lucinda. *From Panic to Power*. New York: Quill,
1995.

Bloch, Douglas. *Listening To Your Inner Voice*. Minneapolis:
CompCare, 1991.

———. *Positive Self-Talk for Children*. New York: Bantam
Books, 1993.

Boldt, Laurence G. *How to Be, Do or Have Anything*.
Berkeley: Ten Speed Press, 2001.

Canfield, Jack and Hansen, Mark Victor. *Dare to Win*. New
York: Berkley Books, 1994.

Cleghorn, Patricia. *The Secrets of Self-Esteem*. Boston:
Element Books, 1996.

Cox, Danny and Hoover, John. *Seize the Day*. New Jersey:
Career Press, 1994.

Evers, Anne Marie. *Affirmations: Your Passport to Happiness*.
Vancouver: Affirmations-International Publishing,
1989.

Helmstetter, Shad. *Self-Talk for Weight Loss*. New York: St. Martin's Press, 1994.

———. *The Self-Talk Solution*. New York: Simon and Schuster, Inc., 1987.

———. *What To Say When You Talk To Yourself*. New York: MJF Press, 1986.

———. *Who Are You Really And What Do You Want?* Park Avenue Press, 2003.

Manz, Charles C. *The Power of Failure*. San Franciso: Berrett-Koehler Publishers, Inc., 2002.

Martorano, Joseph and Kildahl, John. *Beyond Negative Thinking*. New York: Avon Books, 1989.

McGraw, Phillip C. *Self Matters: Creating Your Life From the Inside Out*. New York: Simon & Schuster, 2001.

McWilliams, Peter. *You Can't Afford the Luxury of a Negative Thought*. Los Angeles: Prelude Press, 1995.

Peale, Norman Vincent. *The Amazing Results of Positive Thinking*. Brooklyn: Fawcett Crest Books, 1953.

Proto, Louis. *Be Your Own Best Friend*. New York: Berkley Books, 1993.

Stoop, David. *Self-Talk, Key to Personal Growth*. Grand Rapids: Fleming H. Revell, 1998.

Ventrella, Scott. *The Power of Positive Thinking in Business*. New York: The Free Press, 2001.

Young, Steve. *Great Failures of the Extremely Successful*. Los Angeles: Tallfellow Press, 2002.

ARTICLES

Braiker, H.B. (1989). "The Power of Self-Talk." Psychology Today, December, pp. 23-27.

Fletcher, J.E. (1989). "Physiological Foundations of Intrapersonal Communication." In Roberts & Watson (Eds.), Intrapersonal Communication Processes (pp. 188-202). New Orleans: Spectra.

Grainger, R.D. (1991). "The Use—and Abuse—of Negative Thinking." American Journal of Nursing, 91(8), 13-14.

Korba, R. (1989). "The Cognitive Psychophysiology of Inner Speech." In Roberts & Watson (Eds.), Intrapersonal Communication Processes (pp. 217-242). New Orleans: Spectra.

Levine, B.H. (1991). Your Body Believes Every Word You Say: The Language of the Body/Mind Connection. Boulder Creek, CA: Aslan.

McGonicle, D. (1988). "Making Self-Talk positive." American Journal of Nursing, 88, 725-726.

Pearson, J.C., & Nelson, P.E. (1985). Understanding and Sharing: An Introduction to Speech Communication (Third Edition) Dubuque, IA: William C. Brown.

Shedletsky, L.J. (1989). Meaning and Mind: An Intrapersonal Approach to Human Communication. Bloomington, IN: ERIC Clearinghouse on Reading and Communication Skills. [ED 308 566]

Weaver, R.L. and Cottrell, H.W. (1987). "Destructive Dialogue: Negative Self-Talk and Effective Imaging." Paper presented at the Speech Communication Association Meeting. [ED 290 176]

WEBSITES

www.shadhelmstetter.com
Self-Talk programs on CDs, online goal tracking and motivation, Dr. Helmstetter's books, and Life Coach Certification programs.

www.howtoreprogram.com
Self-Talk and motivational tapes and CDs, Books, Personal and Business Coaching,

www.livingwelltools.com
Self-Talk CDs and resources.

www.thinkrightnow.com
Self-Talk CDs and software.

Quick Order Form

Please send _____ copies of *How To Reprogram Yourself for Success*, at $11.95 per copy, to the address below. I understand I may return any copies for a full refund at any time, as long as they are in resalable condition. **Write to us for quantity discounts.**

Name _____

Address _____

City _____

State / Zip _____

Telephone _____

email address _____

Shipping: Add $4 for the first book and $2 for each additional book.

Payment: ☐ Check or ☐ Credit Card

Card # _____

_____
Name on card

Exp. date: _____ / _____

Mail to: Global Publishing Company, 8436 Denton Hwy, Ste. 208-141, Fort Worth, Texas 76148

www.howtoreprogram.com
E-mail: patrick@howtoreprogram.com

Quick Order Form

Please send _____ copies of *How To Reprogram Yourself for Success,* at $11.95 per copy, to the address below. I understand I may return any copies for a full refund at any time, as long as they are in resalable condition. **Write to us for quantity discounts.**

Name _____

Address _____

City _____

State / Zip _____

Telephone _____

email address _____

Shipping: Add $4 for the first book and $2 for each additional book.

Payment: [ ] Check or [ ] Credit Card

Card # _____

_____

Name on card _____

Exp. date: _____/_____

Mail to: Global Publishing Company, 8436 Denton Hwy, Ste. 208-141, Fort Worth, Texas 76148

www.howtoreprogram.com
E-mail: patrick@howtoreprogram.com